Prep for Rail

i

KC-135 AIR REFUELING F-105S OVER LAOS F-105'S IN FORMATION

H-53 CLASS GRADUATION PICTURE-NEW JOLLY

GREENS

HC-130 AIR REFUELING AN H-53 OVER LAOS

H-53 RAMP GUN, CHECKED BY PJ, SSGT WAYNE FISK

H-53 BATTLE DAMAGE DURING BOXER 22

MISSION

BOXER 22B, LT W. BERGERON, SURVIVOR
LT.COL LYLE'S LAST FLIGHT AT NKP
FAREWELL DINNER AT NKP

AIR REFUELING WITH AN HC-130

LT. COL. YORK AND MARTY DONOHUE AT LIMA SITE 98

P.136 - I was at that Reunion in Dallas - quite emotional

especially when Talking To some of The POW's and how "The Raid" saved many when viets moved Them Together

PROLOGUE

It feels like we've been in this rice paddy forever, but it's only been a few minutes. Sgt. Hodge's pinpoint shooting took out the gun tower outside of my window. I can see several buildings that his gun also set ablaze burning outside of the prison walls. The "Blueboy" Special Forces element should have had enough time to get the American prisoners of war out of their cells and over to the southwest corner of the compound for the Air Force Jolly Greens to come and take them home. What happened to Lt. Col. Britton's helicopter? Did we lose them? Why did the Army guys call for backup Plan Green? I see a lot of SAMs going off, and it's still quiet in the compound. They should be calling for Apple 4 and then 5 to come in and load up our POWs. Nothing . We are to be the last H-53 to go in and take whoever is left back to safety. We did the gunship mission, taking out the guard towers, and next we'll load POWs-- what a mixed mission for our Air Force Rescue Crew. Come on, guys. Our element of surprise is long gone, and it is time to load up and get the hell out of Dodge!

I had just returned from a year's combat tour flying Jolly Greens out of Thailand. I was supposed to be a new instructor pilot at Eglin AFB in Florida. How did I wind up in a North Vietnamese rice paddy just outside of a prisoner of war compound at Son Tay, some 23 miles northwest of Hanoi, at 0230 hours on the morning of November 21? Guess I need to go back and explain a few things...

PREFACE

I was born at the beginning of World War II, in August 1939, in the small town of Sparta, IL. My mother and I stayed with her sister, Katy Simonds, while both my dad (Billie R. Waldron) and Aunt Katy's husband (Lt. Eugene [Gene] Simonds) were in Europe. I remember two small silk flags, white with a blue star in the middle, hanging in the living room window. My dad talked about seeing men in pajamas looking like death warmed over near a place in Germany called Dachau. Neither of them wrote down any of their experiences. I just heard a few stories now and then. I regret not encouraging them to put down in words what they saw and felt during those dangerous times.

Further back, two great, great grandfathers fought with Illinois Regiments during the Civil War. One was Henry Waldron, born in England in 1825. He fought with Gen. Grant at Vicksburg. The other was Martin G. Williamson, who died on April 22, 1862, at the beginning of the Civil War (from illness while on active duty). His grandfather was from near Nashville, TN, so his roots were in the South, yet he was in the US Army of the North. Neither man wrote anything down about what conflicts they might have been in during the war.

In 1969 and 1970, it was my turn to experience the phenomenon of war; the war in Southeast Asia called the Vietnam War. As an ex-fixed wing pilot now flying giant rescue helicopters (H-3 and H-53 Sikorsky's), my daily life changed in many ways.

I am writing about several missions that I flew, some of which I lost friends on. At the end is my personal recollection of my time flying to a place in North Vietnam called Son Tay, a Prisoner of War camp, some 23 miles northwest of Hanoi. That will always be a night to remember.

I want to offer special thanks to old friends from that era--pilots Robert Martin, Ron Olsen, and Wade Weeks ; Pararescuemen Doug Horka, and James (Jim) Rogers. Their input was valuable to me in filling in some details. Technical help from Daniel Pincu and Kyle Engelking was greatly appreciated. Brothers Ed (editing) and wife Sandy (editing), and Terry (cover art) were also a great help. Cover photo courtesy of Jim Rogers.

Chapter I

IN THE BEGINNING

I graduated January 27, 1962, from Clemson University with a degree in civil engineering. I also completed the USAF Reserve Officer Training Corps (ROTC) and became a 2nd Lt. in the USAF. My roommate, James A. Eddings, and I came from Carbondale, IL, to attend Clemson, and, we both wanted to be USAF pilots. Jim's eyesight was less than 20/20, so he went into civil engineering. I had gotten married my last semester in school, but still spent time with Jim as we had our classes together. After graduation, I had six weeks before going into pilot training. I had bills to pay, so I interviewed Proctor and Gamble, and the Tennessee Valley Authority (TVA). TVA hired me, so it was off to Knoxville, TN. My salary was a whopping $525/month. No, I was not on food stamps. Rent was $75/month, and so was my car payment, and you could fill up a shopping cart and get change back from a 10-dollar bill.

After a short six weeks with TVA, the Waldrons headed to Enid, OK. On March 9, 1962, I became a 2nd Lt. on active duty. I was a member of USAF undergraduate pilot training class 63-F, with a proposed graduation date of March 1963. (I believe my base pay at that time was $222.22, with $100 a month flight pay and $75 in housing.)

USAF undergraduate pilot training was one year of very extensive training. The first six months were in the Cessna T-37 side-by-side trainer with dual jet engines. Its nickname was the "tweety bird" since the engines had a high pitch. Without ear protection, your hearing could degrade very quickly. We flew in the morning and had class in the afternoon, or vice versa.

Each student had to solo after 10 hours of dual instruction or face elimination, and we did lose several students who failed to solo. I then transitioned to the T-33, nicknamed "the T-bird." On September 13, 1962 a new addition joined our family- David Ross Waldron. David was the first boy born to anyone in our class after a several new baby girls.

T-33 flying was very intense; especially formation flights when you were number four flying solo with a tough lead instructor pilot who could make you perspire a bit. There were several international students from Iran and Afghanistan. I don't know how they were able to transition to a new language and culture, and yet fly a high performance aircraft. In their culture, they read their books from back to front and right to left.

On one occasion, during a coffee break, one of the Iranian students had a puzzled look on his face while thumbing through his English dictionary. I asked him, "Mohamed, what are you looking for?"

"I can find one word, but not the other," he said.

"What word?" I asked.

"I can find the word 'bull,'" he said, "but I can't find 'bullshit.'"

Our US instructors often used slang, and that sure gave the foreign guys a setback. I could not imagine going to Iran and learning Arabic and flying with one of their guys.

I had a close call while flying a T-33 aircraft during early '63. One night after a cross-country navigation flight, we were returning to Vance AFB for landing. We were coming in from the west, and I was flying in the rear seat. We had flown some instrument approaches with a hood device that kept me from looking outside the aircraft. Once that instrument portion was over, I could pull the hood back so I could once again see outside the aircraft. As we came in for landing, the IP and I both looked out to the north for any traffic on downwind.

"Clear left," said the IP.

I looked out the same direction (it was very clear night) and repeated, "Clear left." Suddenly, I pulled back on the stick and began a climbing turn to the right while giving the T-33 full throttle!

"What the hell are you.... oh my God! Where did he come from?" the IP shouted.

In a wink of an eye, another T-33 suddenly appeared on our left. I saw red and green wing tip lights. Thank God for good eyes and quick reflexes. The pilot in the other T-33 descended and turned to the left. We narrowly averted a mid-air collision.

For a whole year, we flew and studied to complete our training requirements and receive our wings. I was to be the first in my family to get Air Force wings.

During the year, each student took exams in academics and had flying evaluations. At graduation there was an official "class standing" that could determine your future pilot assignment. Before the actual list came down, each of us planned what we wanted to fly and where we would like to go. The top two in the class normally went into a fighter aircraft, and two of our new pilots did go to fighters. I wanted to be a bomber pilot in the B-52. But there were none on the list, so I selected the KC-135 jet tanker assigned to the Strategic Air Command (SAC), with a squadron at Lockbourne AFB, Ohio, near Columbus. Before joining a SAC squadron, however, I had to complete several schools, including survival and KC-135 ground and flight schools. After visiting relatives in Illinois, another pilot training graduate, 2nd Lt. Dennis Boston, and I drove out west in my 1962 Ford. There were no freeways, and cattle were often on the road at night.

One night we arrived at Luke AFB in Glendale, AZ. We stayed overnight for $5 in the BOQ, and then continued to Stead AFB in Reno, NV, to attend basic USAF Survival School. The class work was followed by a week in the Sierra Nevada Mountains. Staying overnight outside in the winter's snow was a once in a lifetime experience--do it once and that is enough. We paired off and had to find our way through the mountains to various checkpoints. At the end of this training, we got to be prisoners of war. This would be my only real experience with how to handle interrogations. I was not sure how I would respond if someone were busy breaking bones in my body.

After survival school graduation, it was off to Castle AFB for ground school and flight simulator training. For actual KC-135 flight training, we went to the famous Walker AFB in Roswell, NM. (I did not see any aliens during this time!)

The first time I flew in the co- pilot's seat and prepared to land the big airplane, my landing was perplexing. As I approached the runway, I slowly brought back the control column, waiting for the wheels to touch, and they did. I heard a noise and said something like, "What is that?"

"It's your landing gear," the instructor pilot replied.

I thought that I was about 50 feet in the air when the noise occurred. It seems my 50 feet equaled zero. My IP found the event very humorous. Next time around I was ready for the noise, and I made a great landing.

Finally, I was certified in the KC-135 as a co-pilot and was off to Columbus, OH. I was part of a combat crew in the KC-135 tanker in the Strategic Air Command: pilot, co-pilot, navigator, and boom operator.

We were given a crew number, R-150, and spent a lot of time flying and being on alert. (This concept of flying with the same guys would change later in my flying career.) Often, our crew would head north to Goose Bay, Labrador, Canada, to "pull alert" for a week. Our aircraft would sit there with 20 others, all loaded with JP-4 jet fuel, ready to launch in a few minutes to air refuel B-52s on their way to Russia. Alert status meant that crews would pack up a suitcase for a week's tour on their US base or in Canada. Each crew was assigned an aircraft, and it was checked out up to the time to start engines. If we went to war, we had a limited amount of time to get all of the aircraft off the ground before a missile or bomb could take out the base. We often had practice launches where we would start engines and taxi to the runway; we just did not take off.

After three years in Ohio, the USAF transferred several crews to Kokomo, IN, home of Bunker Hill AFB. The Waldrons bought their first house there, all of $19,000 for a three-bedroom house with garage. David started school there, and on July 14, 1967, Jon Thomas Waldron joined the clan.

That fall I had my first long temporary duty (TDY), which took our tanker crew all the way to Utapao Air Base near Sattihip, Thailand. During our time there, I accumulated several hours flying combat missions refueling USAF fighters and B-52 bombers that were attacking targets near Hanoi, North Vietnam. On some missions we would refuel the fighters on their return to their home base; often one of the fighters would not make it back. On occasion a crew was shot down, and the pilot and/or navigator might be captured or killed. On one flight I had my old 8mm camera on the flight, and the boom operator filmed the fighters coming in to air refuel. I was awarded an Air Medal for my missions flown. On return from our time out of country, we landed at our home base shortly after midnight. The tower called us, "Congrats, Lion 42. You are the first crew to land at Grissom AFB, the new base name."

By early 1968 I had over 1500 hours flying time in the KC-135, and I was placed in the aircraft commander upgrade program, which required an in- flight check by the head flight examiner before you were cleared to have a crew under your command. Then you and your crew went before a review board headed by the Vice-Wing Commander, and they put you under intense questioning to see how you and your crew would respond under pressure. We passed! I was now responsible for three other lives and a $3 million aircraft.

My crew: Capt. Thomas Waldron, Aircraft Commander; First Lt. Jim Hughes, co-pilot; Capt. Allen Skinner, navigator; and MSgt. Frank Brown, boom operator.

Toward the end of 1968, my crew headed off to the Southeast Asia war zone flying missions out of Okinawa, Thailand, and Formosa. We would fly air refueling missions with bombers and fighters, day and night.

Near the end of our 60-day tour, we had a night refueling flight with four F-4s over Thailand, east of

Bangkok. After completing our offload, we turned and headed south to Utapao. Co-pilot Lt. Jim Hughes noted that the oil pressure reading on number three engine (the inside engine on the right side) was fluctuating.

Jim looked up the situation in our flight manual and said, "Sir, our oil pressure is near the point where we would have to shut down the engine."

We quickly had MSgt. Brown come up and replace the # 3 gauge with the #2 gauge. This would confirm if we had a problem or a bad gauge indicator. As luck would have it, the # 3 gauge was working properly. Within a few minutes, the limits were approaching shutdown time. The navigator was monitoring this very closely. I don't think he had ever flown in a KC-135 with an engine shut down, well, neither had I.

The time came to shut down the number three engine. "Jim," I said, "confirm the number three throttle and place your hand on it." (In the past, pilots had been a little lax and actually shut down a good engine.)

I confirmed he indeed had the number three throttle handle. I slowly brought the handle back until it stopped at the position called "flight idle." If the oil pump were to fail, it is possible the engine could blowup--not a good thing! Once I raised the engine handle and placed it in the shutoff position, there was a slight yaw action. The nose moved toward the right since there was now an "extra" engine on the left side, which produced a turning action toward the right. A little left rudder resolved the problem.

Next was our radio call. "Dressy Lady, this is Blue Anchor 43 declaring an emergency. We have shut down number 3 engine." (Dressy Lady was a control site that monitored aircraft movement like our civilian FAA).

"Roger, Blue Anchor 43. Are you bailing out?"

"No sir," I replied. "I still have three more engines!"

We were cleared to proceed directly to Utapao Air Base. As we came in for a landing, I noticed several ground vehicles with red lights rotating. I greased the big bird onto the runway.

As we rolled out, the navigator said, "Boy, you sure made a great landing!"

"I had to," I said. "Look at all the people out there watching!"

After the other engines were shut down, our crew chief came onboard the aircraft. "Sir," he said, "good thing you shut that engine down. There is a lot of oil leaking. If you'd waited a bit longer, the engine might have exploded!"

We completed over 30 combat missions and a few hundred flying hours, and I received another Air Medal. I had been an aircraft commander for a year and had nearly 2,000 hours in the KC-135. For a 30- year-old guy, things looked good. In fact, after our return, my boss called me into his office and told me I was selected to upgrade to an instructor pilot in the KC-135 tanker. That would have been a great career move at my age: an instructor pilot in SAC at the age of 30.

I had completed two 60-day temporary duty assignments, once as a crew co-pilot and the latest with my own crew. I was awarded two Air Medals for the combat flights we made over Thailand and Laos. My flying career was looking good and predictable.

But the next week, I was called in by my commander again. "It looks like things have changed," he said. "The Air Force is sending you to helicopter training school in Texas, and then on to Udorn Air Base, Thailand, as an HH-53 pilot, the super Jolly Green rescue helicopters."

Wow, helicopters in a war zone? Me? Could this be true? How would I tell the family? The war now became very personal. I was about to get a lot closer to bullets and bad guys...So much for my plans.

I suspect that the USAF was in a bind. They had the mission of combat rescue in Vietnam and Laos. Until this war, there had not been many USAF helicopter pilots graduated, as the demand was low. But since the goal was a one-year tour, something needed to be done to bring in more new helicopter pilots. They could not be rookies, because they would be placed into a combat role that needed experienced pilots. The USAF made a decision to tap KC-135 and C-141 aircraft commanders with a year's experience as aircraft commanders to fill the helicopter positions. So much for SAC; so long KC-135, so long family. Looks like I'll be in a combat zone for the year to come.

We sold the house in Kokomo, packed up the1967 Ford, and headed south to Wichita Falls, Texas, home of Sheppard AFB. There I would learn to fly the Bell H-1 single engine helicopter and the dual engine Sikorsky H-3. That was when I met a couple of guys who would become lifelong friends: Maj. Robert Martin (we called him Maj. Bob), and Capt. Ron Olsen.

Before heading to Thailand, there was one more stop, Eglin AFB in Destin, Florida, home of ARRTC-the Aerospace Rescue and Recovery Training Command. This was our last stop to train on yet another helicopter, the Sikorsky H-53, the Super Jolly Green. It weighed 40,000 pounds with full fuel and armament. (By contrast, the H-3 weighed only 20,000 pounds.)

Our instructors had flown many hours of combat in Southeast Asia. We learned a lot in the next months-- especially how to get into an area and get out in one piece. We were also checked out in a new procedure, air refueling behind an Air Force C-130 Hercules. It was a four-engine turboprop that had been modified with two pods under each wing. Each pod had 75 feet of hose with a "basket" attached. Our task: extend the refueling probe on the right side of the H-53 to just beyond the rotor blades, and maneuver into place to connect and then slip up on the C-130 wing and fill our H-53 fuel tanks with JP-4.

The H-53 flight instructors who taught us those things were Lt. Col. Warner Britton, the overall unit commander; Lt. Col. Jack Allison, our H-53 type helicopter commander; and Maj. Marty Donohue, who was one of my flight instructors. (By year's end I would be flying with these officers into the most heavily defended area in the world--Hanoi, North Vietnam--in an attempt to rescue USAF and USN pilots and crewmembers during a raid on the Son Tay Prisoner of War camp.)

First, though, it was another school, where we learned about new engines, hydraulic systems, electrical systems, flight controls, mini-gun operations, hoist operations, and new crew communication. I also had new aviators on board, no navigator or boom operator. The new guys on our flight crew were the flight engineer and my favorite group of USAF professionals, the pararescuemen or "PJs". (At the time, there were only men in the combat assignments. There are many web sites about the PJ's covering their intense training, and their many deeds around the world. If you see one today, they wear a maroon beret, stop and thank them for their service.)

Little did I know that I was training with men who I later would label as heroes: other pilots, flight engineers, who stood in an open door operating a hoist to bring up a downed pilot, and the PJs on their mini-guns or being lowered to the ground to aid a downed pilot who may be wounded. All of this while the enemy was firing their many weapons: AK-47s, anti-aircraft guns (23mm and 37mm), and the feared hand-held SAM (surface to air missile). And, there was always the possibility of an attack by a Russian MIG 21. Many would pay the supreme sacrifice, losing their life while attempting to save another.

" That others may live" is the motto of the ARRS-Aerospace Rescue & Recovery Service. The main difference in our rescue crew structure was that for each mission you might fly with different crewmembers. Since everyone was certified in his position, it did not matter who was your co-pilot or engineer or PJ that day. This concept made it a bit easier to schedule flights in combat. (I must admit that after awhile I did have my favorites, one being PJ Doug Horka).

The procedure used to rescue a downed airman is to "hover" the large helicopter 20 to 50 feet above the survivor on the ground. The flight engineer in the door would hook a two-foot, metal jungle penetrator onto a cable and lower it with his hydraulic control box to the ground. If the penetrator was in the airstream awhile, it could build up a static charge, and if the person on the ground reached up to grab it he could get quite a shock. The survivors had been told to let the penetrator touch the ground before grabbing on to it, but I bet if someone were shooting at me, I would not worry about a shock.

This device could hold up to three people at one time. Small seats could be pulled down and a strap wrapped around you. When the thumbs-up sign was given, you would be pulled up. If the person on the ground was injured or wounded and unable to move, the PJ could be lowered down to aid the survivor, often under fire. These guys were, indeed, heroes.

Our training time came to an end, and on October 3, 1969, we graduated from H-53 school. We were now Jolly Greens! We were among a select group of airmen who are dedicated to bringing home their brothers-in-arms. Now, it was on to Udorn AFB, Thailand, with a short stop at "Snake School" at Clark AFB, the Philippines.

Chapter II

SNAKE SCHOOL- CLARK AFB, PHILIPPINES

After relocating my family in Charleston, SC, and getting son David signed up in a new school, it was time for me to pack up and head to Oakland, CA, where I would board a contract flight to Clark AFB in the Philippines. All Southeast Asia bound USAF crewmembers were required to complete a jungle survivor school. The students called it "Snake School". It was designed to show us the many booby-traps that were used by the North Vietnamese and the Viet Cong who were fighting in the South against our forces. And, more importantly, how to avoid falling into one!

On the first day of survival class, I was in the middle row about halfway to the rear of a large classroom with an unusual decor. I looked around the room and saw hundreds of names on the walls--too many to count. "Attention," was the command from someone. All students stood at attention as the school's commander entered to give his welcome speech.

"Gentlemen, welcome to Clark," the commander said. "During your break I hope that you look at the names you see on these walls. You have something in common with each one. They also sat where you are sitting. After they completed this course and went to fly in Southeast Asia, they were shot down and either killed, missing-in-action, or captured and thrown into a cell somewhere in North Vietnam. What you learn here may keep your name off my walls. Good luck and God speed."

I knew two of the guys whose names were on his board, Capt. Robert (Bob) Coady and Capt. Monte Mooreberg. Both were in my pilot training class 63-F at

Vance AFB, Ok, graduating March of 1963. They had been listed as missing-in-action for several months.

I don't remember in my thirty years of living a more powerful attention getter. I would soon learn a few lessons that I would take with me to the combat zone, and, hopefully, if needed, they would work. In addition to days of classes, we often went into the field to examine traps the bad guys would set.

Finally, it was time to go into the jungle with a group of natives, the Negritoes. Their relatives had helped our army against the Japanese during World War II. They were very small in build, and they had an innate ability to live off the jungle--things a kid who grew up in Illinois never experienced: how to find water in a plant and how to use a cane section with water added to rice to cook a great supper. Those guys were very unusual in their approach to life; they made survival look easy.

On day two, our job was to be able to conceal ourselves in a jungle area. For a demo, two of the Negritoes hid in a field, and we were to find them. After our group of twenty guys stomped all over the field, with no success, the instructor asked them to stand up. They did, and they were just under our feet. How did they do it? I would have liked to take them along, just in case we were shot down somewhere and had to hide in the jungle.

For our "final exam," our class spent a night sleeping in the jungle. (This included various uninvited critters.) We were simulating being shot down and the need to hide and spend the night and avoid capture. Our hunters were the "friendly Negritos". If they found us, we had to give them a metal "dog tag" we had. They could turn the tags in for a pound of rice per tag. We each had three tags, and you would like to have at least one left after the night to pass the test.

The NCO (non-commissioned officer) in charge gathered all of his students. "Gentlemen," he said, "I am passing out these C-rations (like those used in World War II). That is your dinner. Oh, and by the way, there are many jungle rats in our area. If one bites you, you will need to take the series of shots for rabies. And finally, don't walk around at night. There are 200-foot drop-offs. So, are there any questions?"

Our instructor departed, and we began to seek out hiding places in the brush. I could see where some of the guys were hiding, just in case I needed to get away from any critters lurking around. It was still light when I finished the chow and realized that the crumbs I generated could provide an incentive for a visit from a rat and his friends. I used some of my drinking water to clean up my very greasy hands.

It was going to be a long night. I had never heard anyone snore in the jungle. It was amazing when I heard Maj. Gill begin sawing Zs. Hah, I thought, I bet he gets caught by the Negritoes. Just about the time I was nodding off, I heard several rats running about in the brush. Damn, they sounded big! Really big! I decided to keep one eye open during the night.

A few minutes went by, and I heard a new noise. This noise was familiar: mosquitoes. They were a bit larger than those in Illinois and Florida. I pulled out the plastic bottle of 6-12 and spread the stuff on my arms and face to keep the bugs away. I was ready for what was to come. And they did. I heard a noise, someone walking and sniffing. The 6-12 was acting like perfume, and a Negrito guy came right up to my spot. I handed over one of my dog tags. One dog tag was gone; two were left. Within five minutes I heard another walker-sniffer. He was coming for his metal dog tag for rice. I guess the guys worked in pairs. The rats were still running about doing whatever rats do at two am.

After a very long night, I heard a really great sound, a rooster crowing. Great, those guys usually crow at sunrise in all the western movies I had seen. I don't know why, but I checked my official Air Force watch. It read three o'clock, and it is way before sunrise. If I could have found that rooster, it would have been his last day to crow.

The night finally ended. A rescue H-3 helicopter came to take us back to the base: a shower, real food, and a nice, soft bed. I never thought that something we take for granted every day could become a luxury.

I realized that if I had been shot down, I might still be in the jungle evading enemy soldiers. Instead of handing someone a "rice chit," the soldiers would either shoot me or tie me up and drag me off to a prisoner of war camp. Yes, I did learn something, and I hoped I never had to use it. I would never look at 6-12 in the same light. It was now a perfume.

School days were over, and it was off to Thailand, first Bangkok and then on to Udorn Air Base in the northern part of Thailand. I understood that where we were going to work was not a friendly place. Actually, it was a place that could become quite lethal in a very short time.

During World War II, it was said there were no atheists in foxholes. In the Vietnam War, I don't think there were too many atheists in cockpits, either.

Chapter III

ONWARD TO THAILAND

Once again my bags were packed, and it was off to Bangkok, Thailand. In Bangkok, the USAF shared runways with the commercial side, the Air Force operating C-130s and C-141s. The C-130s made a circuit of all five bases in Thailand, taking people and supplies to those outposts.

The military also operated a hotel in Bangkok called the Choa Phya Hotel. During the drive to the hotel, I noticed the cars were driving on the left side. I guess they got that from the Brits. Since I was not driving a vehicle, I never gave it too much thought. However, there was an incident involving a Yank who went out of his hotel to find a cab. While looking to his left, he stepped into the street and was struck and killed by a car coming from his right. (I remembered that in London they have signs telling the pedestrian to "look right".) That was a heck of a way to get killed while out of the war zone.

The USAF had five major air bases located throughout Thailand. In the center were Korat AB, home to the F-105s and B-57s (including some Aussies), and Ubon AB, home of the F-4 night- fighters. To the east was Nakhon Phanom AB (NKP), home of the A-1 sky-raiders; A-26s (night-fighters); various forward aircraft control aircraft, such as the OV10s, O-1s and O-2s; and Detachment 1, 40th ARRSq, home of the Sikorsky H-3 rescue helicopters, nicknamed "nit-noy Jolly Greens". (Nit-noy in Thai means small.)

To the north was Udorn AB, home of many F-105s and the Thailand Air Force's T-28s. My new squadron, the 40th ARRSq, was also located there, with about a dozen

Sikorsky H-53s, the "Super Jollys". "Air America" also had aircraft and old helicopters stationed there at times.

On the far southern end of Thailand was Utapao AB, near Satihip. SAC aircraft-KC-135 jet tankers and the giant B-52s, used it. I had flown many flights from there in the KC-135. Some 35 miles north of Udorn AB is Vientiane, the capital city of Laos.

Why were these Air Force rescue helicopters located in northern and eastern Thailand when this was the "Vietnam War"? At this time in 1969, the USAF and USN/USMC aircraft were bombing trucks and infantry using the roads to take supplies through the Mu Gia pass from North Vietnam into Laos, and eventually down into South Vietnam. If an F-4 or F-105, both common USAF attack fighters, or a USN A-4 (Senator John McCain's aircraft type), or an A-6 from offshore carriers was hit by a surface to air missile (SAM), or an enemy MIG, the airborne warrior(s) might be forced to eject from a burning aircraft, most often into an area that was not friendly. Our work place was often hostile, since the same guns that shot down the survivor's aircraft were also waiting for the rescue guys to come in their slower helicopters to attempt a rescue of the survivor(s).

Maj. Bob, Capt. Ron, and I all signed in at our new base (Udorn AB) and made our way to settle into our quarters. The "Hootch," as we called it, was shaped like a big H. Rooms were on the "legs" of the H, and in the middle was a large "party" room. There were showers and toilets on each side. Bob and Ron were assigned a room together on the east side of the H. My roommate, Capt. Bill Furst, and I were assigned to a room on the west end of the H. We each had a bunk bed, a small chest of drawers, and, thank God, a window air-conditioner. (I never told my cousin, who was an Army lieutenant sleeping outside in Vietnam.)

The next day it was off to our squadron to get fitted for a parachute, a "bullet-proof" flight helmet, and an explanation of the weapons (an M-16 rifle and a .38 caliber pistol) we would be issued on each flight. We had qualified shooting these weapons while in Florida. Then, there was also the "blood chit". This laminated document was about 12 by 12 inches and had information printed in several languages. It translated into: "Take this US airman soldier to the nearest US Embassy, and you will receive $100 in gold." You folded it to about three by three inches, and it fit into one of your survivor vest pockets. It was a controlled item and had to be checked out each time you flew. It was great to turn it in after a flight; that meant you made it back!

We also met two instructor and evaluation pilots, Maj. Phil Prince and Maj. Al Heeter. We would train with them to learn local flying procedures and combat techniques. Once a pilot had enough experience and minimum flying time, one of these evaluators would give him certification to fly as an aircraft commander with his own crew in combat operations. As pilot evaluators, their job was very difficult. They were your comrades in flying combat missions, but they also had to evaluate each pilot to confirm that he was indeed qualified to be in charge of a combat crew. (During my time, there were a few H-53 co-pilots who never checked out as aircraft commanders. I guess something in them did not make the grade.) A point emphasized on each training flight was that there were not just two pilots in the H-53. There were also a flight engineer and two PJs in the back. It did not take long to appreciate each one of them.

The engineer would normally operate the rescue hoist (called a jungle penetrator) to retrieve a downed airman. All three were qualified to fire the three H-53 miniguns. In some cases, it was necessary to send a PJ down on the jungle penetrator to attend to a downed crewman who was severely injured or even knocked out. These were not routine flights such as those we flew in Florida. In the war zone, there were folks who would like to shoot you and your helicopter out of the sky. The natives in Destin, Florida, were always friendly.

Maj. Bob and I circulated around the squadron and met other pilots and crewmembers, some of whom we had previously met during training time in the states. Capt. Ron and I were assigned an additional duty as Awards and Decorations Officers. Also assigned to work with us was a young PJ. We had no idea how much work that would entail. When a crew or crews were on a mission that our Squadron Commander thought deserved special recognition, the Awards and Decorations guys would have to write up the mission to include as many details as possible, sort of like writing a book. We used electric typewriters with carbon paper between the regular sheets.

Awards for Air Medals, Distinguished Flying Crosses, Silver Stars, and, rarely, an Air Force Cross would be submitted during our time in the war zone. (On my first helicopter flight at Sheppard AFB, Texas, I flew with an instructor, Capt. Gerald Young, who held the Medal of Honor. He had flown UH 1-Fs in Vietnam.)

After lunch, it was time for briefings by personnel from the Tactical Fighter Wing Intelligence Section. Each day, these "Intel Specialists" sorted through lots of data and analyzed various sightings in order to give the flight crews the best information available. On the day you were flying, they could predict what air defenses to expect and just where you would find them. We were all given plastic coated navigation-type maps where we could easily mark known locations of SAM sites and Anti-Aircraft Artillery (AAA) sites, usually 23mm or 37mm in our areas.

The MIG airfields were all located within the North Vietnamese borders. The main one was outside of the capital, Hanoi, code name HOTEL. Another MIG airfield was south of Hanoi at a place called Vinh, code name CRAB. It was close to the border with Laos and South Vietnam. The most difficult type of AAA to locate was the mobile AAA. These guns were mounted on trucks, and they constantly moved around the theater of operations. Damn, smart bad guys!

The major from Squadron Operations also gave a briefing. "Gentlemen, you are all qualified in the H-53 by position--pilot, co-pilot, flight engineer, or PJ. A big difference: while flying in Florida no one shot at you. That is not so here!

"Since some pilots are coming in as co-pilots, you will need to upgrade to aircraft commander within a few months. This is only a year tour, and we need qualified aircraft commanders as soon as possible. After your in-theater checkout as co-pilot and some combat mission flying time, you'll be evaluated by an instructor pilot. Then, if ready, you will be entered in the aircraft commander upgrade program. The PJ's will receive continual training in medical procedures by our assigned Air Force Flight Surgeon."

(I knew that all PJs were qualified to do tracheotomies, administer morphine, and stop serious bleeding to keep a survivor alive and get him back to a hospital. One of our youngest PJs, not yet even an NCO, had recently been awarded the Air Force Cross. That is one award below the Medal of Honor.)

"Let me go over what happens when an aircraft is shot down and the crew has bailed out," the major continued. "Most Air Force and Navy fighters come into an area and work with a Forward Air Controller (FAC). These FACs are pros; they know their assigned target areas like the backs of their hands. They also know enemy AAA gun or SAM locations and the proficiency of each gunner. When someone is shot down, the FAC may be the one who calls in the Search and Rescue request to higher headquarters in Saigon. The air war stops! Every effort will be made to retrieve the downed crew.

"The C-130 aircraft changes its call sign to King and begins to locate airborne resources to use, if needed, in the survivor's area. There might be enemy AAA sites to take out and/or enemy soldiers to neutralize near the survivor. MIGs could also be a potential threat in the immediate area. If so, then USAF/USN fighter aircraft would need to be configured to fight air to air."

The major stopped to sip some coffee and continued. "By that time, our squadron will have received a call to 'Launch the Jollys!' That is your cue to get to your helicopters, start engines, and take off in the direction of the mission. The exact mission location will be given using the closest TACAN navigation site, if possible.

"As you head in the mission direction, your A-1 fighter support aircraft, now called Sandy Lead and Sandy 2, will contact you on your assigned frequency. Since the two Jollys are in formation, we call the lead Jolly 'Low Bird' and the other Jolly, 'High Bird'. Each Jolly will have two A-1 escort fighters. They are your big brothers. The Low Bird is the primary helicopter to make the pickup. The Sandy Lead is the On-Scene Commander and will direct airstrikes against hostile forces. When Sandy Lead determines the rescue area is safe for a rescue attempt, he will notify the lead Jolly, who then receives final information as to the heading and situation of the downed airman. On the run-in to the survivor's location, the A-1s will escort you and take out enemy gun positions. Your PJs will all be on their guns, as will the flight engineer. Within the crew, use your interphone to tell the pilot what you see or need. If you are taking fire and need the pilot to rotate the H-53 while in a hover, he can do that.

"On the final run-in," the major said, "the Jolly Green aircraft commander becomes the On-Scene Commander. It is in your hands. Gents, our job is to keep our brothers from being killed or captured. Don't ever forget that we are all in this together. Your first flight will be scheduled within a few days. I recommend you study your maps and enemy gun locations. Look for defined rock formations in Laos. One might look like a duck, another, a castle. Know them and use them quickly to reference the position of a downed crewman. That is all."

"Wait," he added. "There is something else you will carry on each mission and that is the gas mask." He held one up. "Often, a tear gas is used that makes the recipient sick. It won't kill you, but you won't feel like flying for a bit. Sandy Lead will determine if and when it is used. The code name changes each day. Also, the bad guys have some of our radios they have taken from captives, so they can monitor our guard frequency."

Wow, what a day. After getting settled in and unpacked, I thought that all was on schedule. But I was wrong. Two days later, before getting our first H-53 local training flight, Maj. Bob and I were told to see our Operations Officer, Lt. Col. Frank Catlin. (Bob and I had noted that for a dozen H-53s there seemed to be a lot of pilots assigned--more than 35. We later found a classified study that showed what our anticipated fatality rate was, and it was not good.)

Both Maj. Bob and I, while flying in SAC, had two previous tours of 60 days each in the KC-135 refueling fighters and bombers in Thailand and Laos. We each got half of that time toward our return date from this tour, so our one-year tour became 10 months. Detachment 1, 40th ARRSq at Nakon Phanom Air Base (NKP) who flew the Sikorsky H-3s, are undermanned by two pilots, and the Air Force was not sending any new H-3 pilots to the Detachment.

Since Bob and I both had gone through the H-3 training just before the H-53 training, and we had a few months credited to our year's tour, we became prime candidates for temporary duty at the Det 1, 40th AARSq detachment at NKP, flying in the H-3s. We didn't know if we would be there one, two, or three months. We packed again and caught a flight on a C-130 to NKP, 100 miles due east on the border of Laos. At NKP we found five H-3s and only eight pilots, plus their commander. Maj. Bob and I would be roommates for the next few months. Little did we know what was in store for us in the near future?

Sikorsky Corporation made both the H-3 and the H-53, but there were some big differences. The H-3 weighs 20,000 pounds, has two jet engines, can air- refuel, and has two older M-60 machine-guns, one out of the crew entry door, and other out the opposite window. The Jolly Green crew: two pilots (an aircraft commander and a co-pilot), a fight engineer (FE), and two pararescuemen (PJs).

The H-53 weighs 40,000 pounds, has two larger engines, can also air-refuel, and has three 7.62mm mini guns, six barrels that can fire 2,000-4,000 rounds per minute. The first two guns are located like the H-3, and the third gun is on the rear ramp, which can be opened during flight. The rear gunner, (PJ), stands inside a bulletproof tub that protects him from any piercing rounds that might come from underneath the helicopter. The H-53 pilots had no triggers to fire guns, but we did have a red switch that turned on the guns. The pilot could maneuver the helicopter around a point to enable the crewmembers to fire at any bad guys. There were physical stops on each gun to make sure one of your guns didn't shoot your fuel tanks or tail rotor.

Another big operational difference between the two helicopters was the external fuel tanks. During an attempted rescue where ground fire was possible, the fuel tip tanks could be hit by ground fire. External fuel tanks on the H-53 had fire-suppressant material inside, so if a bullet hit it, the tank would not explode. Not so with the H-3! Without fire-suppressant inside, those tanks could explode and destroy the H-3. So, the H-3 external tanks had to be jettisoned prior to a rescue attempt whenever the threat of gunfire was in play. After that, you were down to less than an hour's flight time if you could not make it to a C-130 tanker.

NKP was a smaller base and easier to get around. Our unit had a small jeep that could take us from our quarters to the flight line. Our H-3's were parked close to the runway, so we could be airborne very quickly. Down the parking ramp I could see A-1s, OV-10s and some A-26s-night fighters. Mission call signs were assigned to each aircraft. The one with tail number 61-17836 was Jolly 74 and another was Jolly 72, etc. The call sign stayed with the aircraft and not the pilot. The A-1s had three squadrons: call signs were Hobos, Fireflies, and Zorro's. They carried different types of ammunition, but always had their 20mm guns located in their wings. The pilots were very accurate and could put bullets very close to some bad guy hiding in the bushes. Once a rescue mission was determined, the A-1s on site changed their call signs to Sandy 1, Sandy 2, and so on. The lead Sandy pilot was On-Scene Commander and would direct the rescue operation. When the lead Jolly Green made his final run-in to make the rescue, he became the On-Scene Commander.

The Forward Air Controllers at NKP used the call signs Nail and Raven. These pilots and crewmembers worked the same geographic area each day and quickly became experts on anti-aircraft artillery (AAA) gun emplacements and the deadly SAM locations. On a rescue mission, FACs directed our fighters to take out the AAA defenses. These FACs often were shot down themselves, due to the dangers associated with their job. If a jet aircraft had a FAC mission, he would have a "Misty" call sign if flying an F-100, or a "Wolf" call sign if flying an F-4. Those jets used a lot of fuel, and they were always looking for a KC-135.

All of the pilots at NKP shared an officers' club, which cost five bucks a month for dues. That was where we ate most meals and downed a few cold beers after a flight. The NCOs also had a club, as did the younger airmen. We did eat off base at times and were surprised at the great French onion soup you could find. Of course, the French had been in Indo- China a few years earlier and influenced some food dishes.

Our living quarters were kept clean by a Thai lady (Piza Mai) and her girls. We paid a few bucks a month to help buy items such as boxes of Tide and scrub brushes. The shower's floor was used as the washing machine. If we smelled bad, it did not matter, since all clothes were washed from the same water source. I guess our noses adjusted.

After Bob and I had once more settled in, it was time to fly the H-3 again.

CHAPTER IV

BACK IN THE H-3, THE NIT-NOY JOLLY

Maj. Bob and I were now checked out by Maj. Ed Robbins to fly as first pilot in non-combat flights and co-pilot on combat flights in the H-3. He emphasized how important our fellow crewmembers were during a rescue mission. The flight engineer who operates the rescue jungle penetrator (the hoist), and the two PJs who are our door gunners were key in any rescue operation. Little did I know at the time that I was in the company of heroes--guys who would stand in a doorway under fire to lower the hoist or the PJ who would get on the penetrator and ride down to a wounded or trapped pilot, often under fire from enemy gunners. During our short training time, we got to meet most of our H-3 crew members; hopefully, we would get to know each one of them before we went into combat.

By mid-November, rescue missions in Laos begin to increase. My friend, Capt. Wade Weeks, flew co-pilot on a rescue mission under enemy fire near the Mu Gia Pass, the main route from North Vietnam through Laos and into South Vietnam. The northern forces would use the route to truck in ammunition, fuel, and other supplies to the Viet Cong and North Vietnamese regulars fighting our troops in the South. The 40th ARRSq H-53's from Udorn AB, our home squadron, were very busy picking up F-4 crewmembers. On November 22, Capt. Ron was copilot on a crew who rescued a Navy pilot. That mission was a bit hectic, as the H-53 overshot the downed pilot and took severe ground fire. They were fortunate not to have any serious damage or injuries.

After Capt. Ron's rescue mission, Maj. Bob and I were at the Officer's Club at NKP. Standing at the bar, talking about that day's mission, were some of the A-1

Sandy pilots, the fighter guys always talked with their hands, so it was easy to pick them out in a crowd. As Bob and I walked up to the group, I noticed a young lieutenant's name tag. In big letters was his last name: Doolittle! He was, indeed, Col. Jimmy Doolittle's grandson. What an honor. The A-1 pilots were concerned that, during the rescue mission, the Sandy lead had overshot the survivor's position as he directed the H-53 Jolly Green on his final approach to the downed pilot. The H-53 then came under small arms fire, but there were no injuries.

I asked, "Has anyone told you that the H-53 weighs twice as much as the H-3 helicopters that you have been working with on earlier missions? Both helicopters' airspeed on the final approach to the survivor is about the same, which means you have a lot more energy to dissipate in the same distance with an H-53 versus the H-3."

One of the A-1 majors replied, "You mean that we need to slow the H-53s down sooner."

I answered, "Yes sir, that should solve the problem."

"I'll get the word out to the other A-1 units," he said.

"Great," I said. I guess no one from higher headquarters had bothered to study the situation and inform the various support aircrews involved during a rescue operation, including the A-1s, the FACs, the Ov-10s, and 0-2s. So, we had to work this out in the field on our own, and we did.

I continued talking to the A-1 pilots. "During our helicopter training," I said, "I had the same experience, and it cost me a beer. On my first approach in the H-53 (previously, I had flown the H-3), the instructor said I bet you a cold beer that you overshoot the landing spot. I said: "You're on."

"As I flew by my intended landing spot some 30 feet high with a forward airspeed of 25 knots, I soon learned that the H-53 was indeed a beast and had to be slowed down sooner. I lost that beer bet. As an engineer, I recalled the old F=MA equation. By golly, it was correct. In the H-53, we have double the mass."

As we finished our evening's chat, I noticed the club jukebox had played two of the A-1 pilots' favorites. One was John Denver's "Leaving on a Jet Plane." And, since the A-1s and A-26s flew many night combat missions, another favorite was Creedence Clearwater Revival's "Bad Moon Rising." When I hear either of those songs, I remember those nights at NKP.

Another Thanksgiving Day away from home came. Somehow, the turkey in Thailand was just not the same. A lot was missing, like family. Your fellow pilots and crewmembers became your extended family, and we did look after one another. Maj. Bob and I were now part of the NKP flying unit, and we were soon put on the daily flight schedule. The war was on, and we were in it!

CHAPTER V

BOXER 22

Turning the calendar to December 1969 was great. Now 1970 is just around the corner. New H-3 crews came to NKP on temporary duty from the 37th ARRSq in Da Nang, South Vietnam.

Normally, one of our NKP co-pilots would fly with one of their aircraft commanders, and vice-versa, and each chopper had one PJ from each location; so, we had a very mixed crew. Most of the PJs knew each other from previous training schools. They were all super guys, so it did not matter who was on with you for the day. The flight engineers were also all top- notch guys. Most of them had maintenance backgrounds and understood the mechanical, hydraulic, electrical, and fuel systems.

December 5, 1969. Maj. Bob was up early as he was on alert duty, flying co-pilot with Capt. Chuck Smith that morning. I was to fly a training mission later that afternoon, so I made my way down to the operations building on the flight line. I liked to stop and watch the A-1s taxi out, four at a time, run up their engines, and then make their takeoff rolls. It was great to hear the sound of those big engines roaring as they lumbered down the runway, waiting for that magic liftoff speed.

I could see Bob's H-3 sitting on the ramp, ready to launch if needed. After a phone call from Saigon, the operation's clerk would turn on his mike and announce: "launch the Jollys!" If someone were shot down, the air war in Southeast Asia would virtually stop while USAF and USN aircrews supported the rescue effort to bring them back safely. No new POWs on our watch!

A little after 10 in the morning, I entered the operations area. A large map was used to track any current rescue missions. The map was not marked. Before each training flight, you still needed to get your flight gear: parachute, combat survival vest (radios and first aid kit), and weapons in case you were diverted from a training flight to an actual combat mission. We were always prepared for the worst-case situation.

The operation's phone rang shortly after 10:30 am and "Launch the Jollys" was the clerk's message. I could see Maj. Bob and Capt. Smith heading toward their chopper. It was Bob's first mission. Slowly, the mission details came into operations. An F-4 had been shot down near a small village in Laos, near the border of North Vietnam. His call sign was Boxer 22. On board was a pilot and his back-seater (guy-in-back or GIB), usually a navigator. They would now be known as Boxer 22A (pilot) and Boxer 22B (GIB). That way the On-Scene Commander would know which crewmember he was talking to during the mission. They would normally use guard channel 243.0 UHF (Ultra High Frequency) or 121.5 VHF (Very High Frequency) to talk to the survivors. All other aircraft in the area could monitor any conversations between the downed crewman and the On- Scene Commander.

As I studied the map location of the rescue site, I suddenly froze. The site, Ban Phanop, Laos, was just on the west side of the famous Mu Gia Pass. It was one of four passes that came from North Vietnam and fed into the infamous Ho Chi Minh Trail on which many trucks and beasts of burden traveled to take ammo, fuel, and other supplies to the Viet Cong and Regular North Vietnamese troops in the south. I quickly pulled out my maps of the area to look for known anti-aircraft sites and SAM sites. Many

34

such sites surrounded the area. It would take a while to silence the anti-aircraft guns.

Immediately, the USAF began to launch strike aircraft, F-4s and F-105s, to take out the AAA guns. We had several rescue crews airborne and standing by in the area. The crews were from Udorn, NKP, and Da Nang, South Vietnam. Also in the area were fighters armed for air-to air fighting against any potential MIG threat in the area. The Russian/Chinese built MIGs could be launched from two nearby areas. One, of course, was the Hanoi area (code name "Hotel"), and the other was an airfield located near Vinh, North Vietnam (code name: "CRAB").

A C-130 ("King" call sign) controlled the mission, keeping track of available incoming aircraft, and they would designate the safe areas where strike aircraft could hold until needed. More KC-135 refueling aircraft were diverted to provide needed fuel in the coming minutes or hours. The USAF was very involved. Not to be left out, the USN was sending strike aircraft from carriers off shore. It was now a total US effort.

We could hear some of the pilot's conversations on our radio receiver in operations. Whoever was not on the schedule was gathered around the radio. We could hear the Sandy Lead: "Jolly 17, understand you are taking severe gunfire, and you are pulling out to the west. Jink, Jolly, Jink!" Damn! That was Maj. Bob's chopper. (Jink is fighter pilots term meanings don't fly in a straight line!)

About 40 minutes later, the first two H-3 Jolly Greens landed at NKP. I went out on the ramp to see if I could help. Bob was walking toward me.

"Tommy," he said, "I did not think we'd get out of that place alive. Those big guns rolled out of the caves and all hell broke loose! We were in a hover at about 50 feet, and then we had to turn the chopper around and head west. I still don't know how they missed us." He was now a combat veteran.

The FACs ran another series of airstrikes and the Sandy lead called in Jolly 72, an H-53. Capt. Ron was flying co-pilot on that one. They, too, got shot at and were heading westward when it happened. A mobile 37 mm anti-aircraft gun opened fire as they flew directly over the gun. Direct hit! The 37mm round exploded on the H-53 cargo hook located just under the center of the aircraft. They landed at NKP as well due to the severe battle damage.

Bob and I walked over to Ron. He was shaking his head back and forth.

"What happened?" I asked.

Ron said, "We went out the same route that we went in, but the 37 site waited until we were leaving to open fire. Thank God they hit the cargo hook and it absorbed the explosion. Every cockpit gauge was in motion; things were flying all over the chopper. Can you believe it? No one in the cabin area or cockpit was hit by flying pieces of metal. The exploded round made a hole in the bottom of the fuselage the size of a card table!"

By the end of the day, more than half a dozen H-53s and a couple of H-3s were hit by ground fire in the rescue area. The bad guys liked to shoot at the six rotor blades, perhaps thinking that by shooting them the chopper would crash. Most of the H-53's could still fly, though a bit rough; once the chopper landed, it was grounded until the main rotor blades were replaced. The supply officer at Udorn had just complained about storing over 40 main rotor blades. But at six blades per chopper, he'd soon run out.

Most of the first day attempts were made to rescue Boxer 22A, the pilot. On the last rescue attempt, the pilot just missed getting on board the H-53, but he revealed his location to the bad guys. Sandy Lead told both the downed crewmembers to settle in for the night, and we'd be back at first light. That meant that rescue crews would be airborne before sunrise so that they would be on station just at sunrise to make a quick pickup. This procedure had worked before.

However, the next day, December 6, 1969, it appeared the bad guys had been busy. First, no reply was made from Boxer 22A. Sandy lead called out for Boxer 22B.

He came up on his radio. "I heard gunshots last night and some screaming," he said. "I moved a bit further west of the small river." The GIB, Lt. Bergeron, was alive and well, and, so far, hidden from the enemy. No word from Boxer 22 A. Was the pilot dead? Was he captured?

Capt. Holly Bell and crew made one of the first attempts that day. His co-pilot that day was Capt. Wade Weeks, a fellow fixed-wing convert. They, too, were hit by ground fire. Someone on the crew was hit, and they were coming back to NKP. The base hospital crew was standing by with doctors and med-techs. When they landed and taxied in, Holly Bell called in: "One of my PJs was hit. He did not make it."

Dead? One of our PJs was shot and was now dead?

Slowly, Holly's crew came into the operations room. I recognized Capt. Weeks and went over to talk with him. He was a bachelor and did not have any brothers or sisters. He and I always got along, since he went to NC State. (They are big rivals of my Clemson Tigers.)

"Wade, I asked, did you bring in your classified package and M-16? "

"No," he said.

""Sit down. I'll run out and get your package and weapons."

As I trotted over to the H-53, I noticed many of the base guys hanging around the chopper. A young PJ inside had been shot and killed in action. Why were these guys looking at the helicopter? I became a bit miffed and went over and began to chew out the lookers. Many out-ranked me, but I did not care. One of the colonels said to me as he left, "You're right, I'm sorry." He turned to the others: "Let's go!" They did.

I climbed in the H-53 and gathered up Wade's personal gear. I looked back. There next to his bulletproof floor pan was the young PJ and the medical crew. Somehow a bullet came through the floor, missed the pan, and came under his helmet. I don't think he felt anything. He was a young airman, David Davison. He was about the same age as my youngest brother, Terry.

This young hero was someone's son, somebody's brother, someone's nephew or friend. He would never be someone's husband or father. This was my first time during combat to see someone who had paid the ultimate price. He gave his life in defense of his country. He did so trying to rescue a comrade in harm's way. He was a hero. I am sorry I did not know him better in his short life. From then on, I made it a point to know my PJs and flight engineers. I knew that they were the most dependable warriors I would meet during my lifetime. We couldn't forget what we saw and had to keep memories alive, but, most importantly, we had to move on to tomorrow. Our friends would expect us to do so.

On the third day, December 7, Maj. Bob had gone back in with Maj. Ed Robbins. They had a 37mm shell go off very close. Bob later said that Robby's ability to handle that H-3 saved the chopper and their lives.

Two new H-53s moved into the area for another attempt to rescue Boxer 22B. Next, it was my turn in the barrel. I was flying with our Detachment Commander, Lt. Col. Joe Lyle. I gave our assigned H-3 a thorough check to insure it was ready for flight. We would be next. We are strapped in awaiting launch.

But, before we lifted off, it happened! Lt. Col. Shipman and Capt. Rich Basket and crew picked up Boxer 22B. They were headed back to NKP. The base commander and others involved in the rescue, gathered with the base medical crew who were waiting to take the rescued lieutenant to the hospital for examination and treatment, if needed.

The H-53 pulled off the runway and taxied up to the parking area. Lt. Woody Bergeron stepped out of the H-53 and walked toward the waiting crowd. He stopped, saluted the base commander, and then he reached into the flight suit pocket on his lower right leg. He pulled out a bag of muddy water.

He turned and handed it to the doctor and said, "I lost my water purification tablets two days ago. I've been drinking this stuff, so you might want to see what is in there." Woody was still thinking, even after all he'd been through. Tonight he would once again sleep in a bed. His thoughts will always be with his pilot-Boxer22A.

More than a dozen choppers received various degrees of battle damage during the rescue attempts, but, most would become airborne again. We could not afford too many of these days in the future. By day's end, the three-day rescue mission was one of the longest of the war to that time. We Yanks just don't give up.

It was then I realized that I was flying among heroes every day. I remembered reading about "giving your life for a brother." I believe it was in the New Testament in the Book of John. I need to read that again.

CHAPTER VI

"BEEPER, BEEPER, COME UP VOICE"

Maj. Bob and I tried to get our lives back in order. Christmas was coming up, and the "care packages" began to arrive. Families were great about sending goodies and fruitcakes. We even had a one- foot Christmas tree with lights. Our Buddhist maids had not seen a Christmas tree, and didn't understand the fuss about gifts. But they did like the fancy metal cans the fruit cakes came in. So they got their first presents: used fancy cake cans. We heard on the Armed Forces Radio Network that President Nixon had issued a cease-fire order for December 25, 1969. It was the only "day-off" from the air war that our group would have during our tour. New Year's Day was warmer in Thailand than I was used to, growing up in the Midwest, and I was back in the saddle January 2, 1970, on alert in the H-3 with a Maj. George.

We were the "low bird" or first to go in on a rescue attempt if needed. After preflight, we settled in for a long day. We checked fuel status, ammo for the M-60 guns, extra water, and ammo for the M-16s and .38 caliber pistol we carried in our survival vests. We also checked out our "blood chits".

If you had not launched during the day on an actual mission, the procedure was to take off about an hour before sunset to allow you to be in a position to make a last minute rescue before the bad guys could get organized. This procedure had worked in the past.

Packed within each crewmember's parachute was a small device that transmitted a signal on radio guard frequency: 243.0 UHF and 121.5 VHF. The theory was that

41

if the person who bailed out was unconscious, you had a chance to find the downed airman by homing in on his beeper signal. The downside was that the beeper blocked out voice communications with all others in the area. The downed crewman would have to reach up and turn off the beacon. Hard to do if you are not conscious! The bad guys could also find the downed airman using their directional radios set to our frequencies.

I was flying co-pilot that day with Maj. George, who had been in country longer than I, but who had not yet been on a combat mission. We were about to change the status for both of us. Flying with us that day was Flight Engineer SSgt. Thayer "Tom" Pope, two PJs, Sgt. Doug Horka, and Sgt. Rick Beasley. I was always impressed with the medical knowledge these young PJs had obtained in a very short time. They could keep you alive with proper medical attention, including performing a tracheotomy to keep you breathing until reaching a hospital. These guys would not hesitate to get on the rescue penetrator to be lowered to the ground to aid a downed airman, often under hostile fire. I had already met a young PJ, not yet a sergeant, who had been awarded the Air Force Cross, just a notch below the Medal of Honor. They wore maroon berets, and they earned every inch of them. The PJs and flight engineers were all heroes in my book.

We often flew different routes to keep the bad guys guessing which way we were heading. There are many limestone formations in Laos. Some looked like other things, such as a duck or a banana, so when you used those features to give your position, others knew very quickly where you were located. That January second, our crew (call sign Jolly 32) had been airborne about 45 minutes, and we were getting ready to head back to NKP to fly some training approaches. Then I heard a call on guard channel.

"Beeper, Beeper, this is Nail 42, come up voice!" I looked at the major and asked if he had heard any "beeps"? Nope. But when he turned the H-3 south, I heard the haunting "beep, beep, beep."

Our A-1 escorts, Hobo flight, now got into the action. "Nail 42, this is Hobo Lead. Do you have a visual?"

"Roger that," he said. "I see wreckage--looks like a USN A-6. And I see a parachute on the ground."

We had no communication with the downed airman; we only heard the Nail FAC. I was trying to plot just where the guy was downed. I soon found the general location and turned to the major.

"This guy is about 20 miles west of Ban Phanop, Laos," I said," the site of the Boxer22 mission which lasted three days in early December. This is not a good place! There are a lot of bad guys in the area."

Suddenly Hobo Lead changed his call sign to Sandy Lead. We were now in rescue mission mode.

"Jolly 32, do you want to attempt a last-light pickup?"

Maj. George looked at me, and we nodded to each other.

"Roger that," the major replied.

Maj. George asked me to do the pre-pickup checklist. The first item was to alert the crew to prepare for a pickup. First, they had to ready the two M-60 machine guns (our only firepower on board).

PJ Doug Horka calmly said, "Guns are ready." Sgt. Pope reported that the rescue penetrator was checked and ready to be lowered. Then I came to the big item: jettison the fuel tip-tanks.

Before I did that, I coordinated with Maj. George, because when those tanks were jettisoned, our H-3 would be down to internal fuel, or about 45 minutes flight time without being refueled by a C-130 tanker.

Those tip-tanks were a big difference between the H-3 and the H-53. The H-53 tip-tanks contained a fire suppressant inside, but the H-3 tanks did not. If an AK-47 round hit our H-3 tip-tanks, they would explode. So they had to go. It was a strange feeling pushing that red button and watching the tips fall away. I noted the time so I could compute our remaining fuel as needed. There were no Exxon gas stations nearby, only bad guys.

As we began our descent into the valley, I thought of the 23rd Psalm, which mentions the "valley of death". I also knew that I was a gunshot away from being in charge. I just said a quiet prayer: "Lord, I don't have time to think or worry about our safety. I have to be of sound mind to make decisions if need be. I am leaving the safety part up to you. Thanks."

As we approached the pickup site, a large wooded area with a road on our left side, we still were not hearing anything from the downed airman.

"Get ready to go down and help the survivor,"

Maj. George said to the PJ behind him, Rick Beasley.

Behind me, PJ Doug Horka was manning his M-60. We had not received any ground fire from the NVA or the Pathet Lao. It was too quiet. Maj. George brought the H-3 into a 20 foot hover and zero airspeed. Sgt. Beasley secured himself to the jungle penetrator and was lowered by Sgt.

Pope to the ground adjacent to the downed pilot. It was still light, but just barely.

I could see the A-1s flying low and checking for any anti-aircraft gun emplacements. So far so good, Sgt. Pope kept us informed about Sgt. Beasley's actions.

"Sir, he is on the ground and looking at the survivor. He's turned him over and he gave me thumbs down!" (That meant, by the PJs evaluation, the pilot was not alive.)

Just prior to that, I noticed what appeared to be smoke from a rifle barrel just off my ten o'clock position.

"Doug," I said, "we are taking ground fire from our ten o'clock!"

"Roger," he replied. I could hear Doug's gun in action just behind me. Then, it happened, very quickly! We had gotten someone's attention at a 37mm anti-aircraft site somewhere behind our location.

"Jolly 32, there is a 37mm gun firing on you, and he is closing in on your position from your rear," exclaimed Sandy Lead. "Get the hell out of there-- now!"

I recognized this Sandy pilot's voice, and if he elevated his voice, I knew we were in big trouble. He normally was a soft-spoken guy.

"Pull him up now," Maj. George shouted to our flight engineer

Sgt. Pope began bringing Rick into the H-3. He was coming up at an angle, but I was sure he saw the shooting coming from our rear. He did not have time to cut loose the pilot and had to abort his attempt.

We moved slowly from our 20 foot hover and began to gain some airspeed.

"Stay down," directed the Sandy pilot. "Don't climb out until I clear you."

All of a sudden the situation had changed. As pilot in charge, Maj. George had made a decision: five lives versus a recovery situation of the probably dead pilot. We moved along the field, gaining airspeed, and still taking enemy gunfire fire from our left, until we reached the point where Sandy Lead told us it's clear to climb and gain altitude.

We were near the end of the field when we started a climbing turn toward the northwest. As I glanced to my lower left, I saw what appeared to be a smaller anti-aircraft gun, a 23mm. It had two barrels side by side, and I could see alternate puffs of smoke as the guns fired. I waited for the shells to hit. They missed. I quickly tuned in the NKP TACAN station to get us a heading home, and to check the distance to the airfield at NKP. I gave Maj. George a heading of 228 to take us back to NKP. Our radio did not transmit on our unit's frequency, but I did manage to contact the NKP tower, and we were cleared to land.

We taxied to our parking spot, and I noticed quite a few of our guys coming out. As soon as we shut down the engines, they walked around the H-3 to check us over. I opened my window and saw Maj. Bob outside.

"Hey, Dufus," he said. "We thought you guys were shot down since we lost radio contact with you. After you gather your gear, come out here and take a look."

I climbed out of the seat, gathered my helmet, parachute, M-16, and stepped out onto the ramp. It was a great feeling to stand on solid ground again. As I walked around the front of the H-3, I saw our crew chief pointing at some bullet holes in our refueling probe. That was close!

Then, Maj. Bob said, "Check this out," his right hand pointing up just above my seat.

I squinted and then I saw a bullet hole about a foot above where my head would have been. That would not be a good way to get a Purple Heart.

The day was almost done. As usual, our PJs had done an outstanding job. They risked everything in an effort to bring back a downed USN pilot. Sgt. Beasley, who had been on the ground, felt badly, but, he knew we had to leave or we would all be lying dead in a Laotian field. When we were debriefed, Beasley told the staff de-briefer that the USN pilot's neck must have been broken when he bailed out. We never saw a second chute, and this was a two-man crew. The bad news was that these guys would be carried as Missing-in-Action, since our PJ was not a medical doctor and could not pronounce the pilot dead. I felt bad for the families left behind who might have hopes of the return of those two crewmen. Such is war. Rules are rules.

So my first combat mission was in the books. We wanted to bring back the deceased pilots. Their families could have at least had closure. It was not to be. It had been an exhausting day and evening. I went to bed hoping I could get some sleep. I didn't think that I would take a bed for granted again, at least not in the near future.

CHAPTER VII

"BANDITS, BANDITS, HOTEL, NORTH"

January moved along. On the 28th, I was on alert with a partial crew from Da Nang, South Vietnam. Capt. Bill Johnson was an instructor pilot, so I rode in the right seat, the normal position for the aircraft commander. If we were launched on an actual mission, then Capt. Johnson would be in command.

We checked out our H-3, including fuel tanks full and ammo loaded. The flight engineer checked out the hydraulic hoist that operates the rescue penetrator. Our PJs ensured they had the medical supplies they might require, including pain meds that had to be signed for and turned back in if not used. They also inspected the ammo tins to be sure we had the required amount for the two M-60s onboard.

Just before leaving our H-3, I noticed a Thailand Air Force helicopter parked next to us, a Sikorsky H-19, an older reciprocating-engine type. It looked like the pilot was going to start his engine. I noticed the pilot talking to his crew chief. He stood by with a fire extinguisher taller than he was. The pilot raised his right hand and moved it in a circle, which indicated he was starting the engine. Immediately, a large flame spewed from the engine exhaust pipe. The pilot was yelling something as his crew chief ran away from the fire, not bothering to look back. Fortunately, the fire went out. I often wondered whether the crew chief that left his post was punished. Would they shoot him? I guess we'll never know.

After a few months of flying in the area, it became evident that the language of combat flying was very different from day to day flying. Many one- word expressions had different meanings from the norm. For example, "Bingo" was not a game. The pilot who said he had "bingo fuel" meant he had just enough fuel to return to his home base without any air refueling. "Winchester" meant that the aircraft was out of bombs and ammo, and it was time to go home.

Another word that I heard on my first flight in a KC-135 several years before, as we escorted several F-104's from California to Da Nang, South Vietnam, was the word "Bandit". It was normally used twice. A Bandit was a MIG. So, you might hear "Bandits, Bandits," then the location where they had become airborne (e.g., Hanoi, North Vietnam, was called "Hotel"). That was followed by a direction, a geographic heading (e.g., north). So the phrase "Bandits, Bandits, Hotel, North" meant a MIG had taken off from Hanoi airfield and was heading north. This transmission was on the guard frequencies, 243.0 UHF, and 121.5 VHF. The transmission would override other frequencies to make sure each aircraft in the area got the warning. However, if you were talking to someone on another frequency, you would hear yourself talking to the other aircraft or ground station and miss the emergency call.

After lunch that day, the two crews on alert (Jolly 19 and our crew, Jolly 17) were considering a short nap and then it happened. The phone in our operations room rang, and the clerk on duty shouted the phrase that always gave us an adrenaline boost: "Launch the Jollys." We dashed out the door and headed to our H-3. We were cleared to start our engines. As the main rotor began to rotate, I turned the radio to our operation's channel to get our mission location. Then, I heard the transmission from operations.

"Jolly 19 and 17, there is an aircraft down and both crewmembers have parachuted. Their call sign is Seabird 02, an F-105. Location is 090 radial at 95 nautical miles from the NKP TACAN."

"Oh, crap!" I said, looking at the map on my left leg.

"What?" Capt. Johnson asked.

"This location, Captain--it is inside North Vietnam!" It became very quiet in our cockpit.

There were two MIG airfields near the downed aircrew. Hanoi was north of the survivor's location, some 250 nautical miles, and south of Hanoi about 125 nautical miles was another MIG airfield at Vinh, North Vietnam. We were soon airborne and flying slightly high and behind Jolly 19. I began to monitor the many radio channels in our cockpit. FM radio was normally used between the two Jollys and our escort Sandy's. Our radio communications with the Ground Control Intercept (GCI) sites were on UHF. That was like talking to air traffic control in the USA. The GCI sites could track all aircraft that emitted certain signals (IFF/SIF) that would give them your position. There were also channels on HF (high frequency) that allowed a crew to talk to higher headquarters in Saigon, which was several hundred miles away.

As we flew east toward the survivor's location, I began to look for "safe" areas to fly in a holding pattern while waiting for Sandy Lead to head into the area where the downed aircrew members were hiding. As "high bird," we would back up Jolly 19; that is, if he had to abort the pickup, then we'd take over.

At each morning's briefing, pilots updated the known locations of anti-aircraft weapons, mainly23mm and 37mm. We always knew that the bad guys would have small arms, especially AK-47s. I circled the AAA areas on my map, and we set up an orbit several miles west of North Vietnam. This was all coordinated with the C-130 "King" aircraft that was nearby. He would start to track resources coming into the area: fighters who could attack the anti-aircraft sites and those who could go after surface-to-air missile sites (SAMs).

Most important to us were the aircraft designated as "MIGCAP". Those fighters were loaded with air-to-air munitions so they could engage and destroy a MIG. In our helicopters, we had no way to determine if we had been locked on to by an enemy MIG or a ground SAM site radar. We were very open to attack and had to depend on others for protection. The mini guns on the H-53 and the M-60s in the H-3 were okay against small arms fire while the Jolly Green was in a hover, but they were not effective against a MIG.

As we circled in our safe area, we could hear Sandy Lead talking to the King control aircraft. " It looks like the bad guys below are gathering up a parachute; maybe one of the crewmembers has been captured," said Sandy Lead.

There was some confusion in the area where the two crewmen had landed. There was no radio contact with either survivor. Were they captured? Were they shot?

Suddenly, over guard frequency I heard, "Bandits, Bandits, Hotel, North!"

I turned to Capt. Johnson and said, "There's a MIG launch out of Hanoi. He was last tracked heading north. I also heard the MIGCAP F-4's check in. I believe they are to the south of us."

We had been out almost 30 minutes when we saw two H-53s coming in above us from the west. They had launched at the same time we did, and they just completed air refueling, and were taking over as "lead Jollys." I heard them check into the area.

"King 1, this is Jolly 71, flight of two."

"Roger, proceed ahead to 30 miles northwest from downed airmen. Sandy Lead is in the area. Maintain 7,000 feet altitude."(We were about 2,000 feet below them at 5,000 feet.)

The terrain where the downed crewmen were located was somewhat mountainous. The H-53s had more power available; their engines were larger and had more power to hover at higher altitudes. So, they took the lead. There was a lot of radio chatter on all frequencies.

"Jolly 19 and 17, you are cleared to refuel with King 3. Contact him on 275.7."

"Roger that," I replied.

Since we were high bird, the lead H-3 Jolly would refuel first, then us. We were at 5,000 feet, well below the other two H-53 Jollys. I could see them crossing from our left. I saw on the flight schedule that Capt. Holly Bell was in the lead H-53. My friend Capt. Jim Blewitt was flying co-pilot in the high bird.

I had not heard any more reports of the MIG that had launched some 10 minutes before. We continued heading west of the rescue area so that refueling would be in a safer area. Jolly 19 took on fuel first, while we followed in loose formation. I was on the radio coordinating our refueling with King 3. He had just finished refueling Jolly 19, and he was circling behind and below us.

Then, a new MIG call: "Bandits, Bandits, CRAB, WEST," a reference to the airfield at Vinh, North Vietnam.

"Damn," I said to Capt. Johnson. "He's here! How did we miss the previous call?"

Our PJ from Da Nang then came on. "Sir, there was an earlier MIG call while you were on the radio talking to King 3 for air refueling!"

"I missed that one!" I said. "Eyes open guys, the MIG is close by!"

"They are hit!" someone yelled on guard channel.

"Who is hit?"

"The lead H-53 Jolly just exploded. It must have been a missile from the MIG. Everyone get on the deck!"

Capt. Johnson began to lower the collective lever, which is between the two pilots, and is the procedure to use in order to lose altitude.

"Sir, the C-130 is below us!" the DaNang PJ yelled on his intercom.

I grabbed the right arm of the pilot with my left hand and yelled, "No!"

Capt. Johnson gave me a questioning look, and then we both saw the C-130 come out in front and below us.

"Damn," he said. "That was close!"

There was another transmission from someone's aircraft: "What heading should we fly?"

It was quiet for a second. "270," I said. "Head west." I could see a river in front of us as we headed westerly.

"Don't follow the river," someone called.

Good advice, since a fighter could look down and see you following a river and shoot you down. We got as low as possible and headed back to NKP. This mission had ended in the worst possible way. We had just lost an H-53 Jolly

Green, call sign, Jolly 71. The six-crew members on board were all gone.

The rest of us landed at NKP without further incident. We went into the operations room and began to debrief. Capt. Jim Blewitt had taped the mission. We listened to it and tried to take notes to see what happened and what could have been changed.

Jim said, "I saw a yellow missile go by my window. I thought that one of the Sandy aircraft had launched it by mistake. Suddenly, off our right was a MIG 21. The MIG pilot looked at me then pulled up to the right and was soon out of sight. Were we next?"

"You know that the other pilot with Holly Bell was Capt. Leeser?" Jim added. "It was his first in- country flight. He was not even supposed to be here until next month. He wanted to get his year started so he could go home sooner."

That day, January 28, 1970, the USAF lost six heroes. Families back home lost sons, husbands, fathers, brothers, and friends. Jolly 71, an H-53 super Jolly Green rescue helicopter, was shot down in hostile territory by an enemy MIG 21. The crewmembers were:

Capt. Holly Bell, pilot;

Capt. Leonard Leeser, co-pilot;

MSgt William Pruett, PJ;

TSgt William Sutton, PJ;

Sgt. William Shinn, flight engineer;

Sgt. Gregory Anderson, combat photographer.

This had been my first time in combat where a whole crew was lost. It was a very somber night for those at NKP and Udorn. (Udorn was home base for Holly's crew and the Seaboard 02, F-105.) That night, we went over the mission in our minds to see what could have been done any differently. What if the MIG had used his other guns to attack or fired more missiles? There were four helicopters and four A-1s nearby that were vulnerable. We could have lost more aircraft that day. The MIGCAP had anti-aircraft batteries between them and the helicopters. They could not respond in time to take on the MIG 21. At speeds of 400-500mph, a lot happens in a short time.

Someone in the squadrons would have to ensure that the families of those lost were notified. Packing up the personal gear of each downed crewmember would begin the next day. I don't recall any time during our training that we even talked about that possibly happening. A lot of us knew the families of the lost crewmen. We had gone through training with them. We had gone on picnics with them and their families. Many good people were lost in this war.

In just a few short months, we had lost seven crewmen. But we still had tomorrow and the next day to deal with. We just did it one day at a time. And we never knew what position we were flying the next day until the afternoon before.

CHAPTER VIII

STILL AT NKP

Spring 1970 was just like most of the other days, except the humidity is a bit lower than in muggy August. Bob and I were beginning to pack things up. We were to head back to Udorn Air Base very soon and become re-certified in the H-53 super Jolly Green helicopter.

There had been another pickup made of a forward air controller (FAC) pilot early that morning. A Jolly Green crew from Udorn picked up the downed pilot and returned there after bringing the survivor back to NKP. A few of us H-3 pilots were sitting around a table at lunch in the Officer's Club, sipping ice tea and discussing the rescue when a young lieutenant came up to our table.

"I see by the patches on your flight suits that you guys are Jolly Greens," he said.

"Yes," several of us answered.

"Well, I know you guys were not the ones who saved me today," he said, " and, I didn't get a chance to say something to the crew who did. What do you even say to someone who saves your life? All I can say is, thanks." He turned and slowly headed out the front door.

We were suddenly very quiet. I guess we knew that our job was to save lives, to bring back downed airmen and keep them out of prisoner of war camps, but we just never talked about it. We did remember that the rescue work we do sometimes costs the lives of our crews. Later that evening there was a knock at our BOQ door. Bob was closest, so he got up and opened the door.

"Hey, Bob," said a major I did not know.

Bob shook his hand, and they both walked over to me. Bob introduced the major, an old friend from pilot training who now flew the A-1. He had taught astrophysics at the USAF Academy. I was impressed. He wanted to discuss a situation he was resolving.

"Bob, do you remember the young A-1 pilot we lost a few weeks ago? Well, I've been assigned to go through his personal effects and send them to his next of kin," he said. "The lieutenant was single, so I guess his things will go to his folks. My problem is some letters I found. They were from a girl. I don't know if his folks knew about her or not. I was thinking I should send those letters back to her, in case it might upset the parents if I send the letters with his personal items. What do you think?"

Bob and I looked at each other and just nodded our heads. He thanked us and got up and left. Sometimes issues can be resolved without saying a word. I guess that was one of those times.

At the end of a quiet week, a few of us on late duty were climbing in Col. Joe's jeep when we heard some sirens go off. We looked over toward the runway and saw an A-1 that had just taken off for a flight turn about and prepare to land. He left his gear up during the excitement, and we suddenly had a Fourth of July gathering on the runway. He was able to get away safely, riding down his parachute, which he activated as soon as he landed. The A-1 had a Martin-Bacon system that allowed the pilot to eject while on the ground at low airspeeds.

He landed on top of the communications shack and seemed to be OK. His A-1 continued to belch flames and set off machine guns and other assorted explosives. The fire department guys decided not to get close until the fireworks show ended. It was quite a mess to clean up before any other flights could get in or out of the base. Handling unexploded ordinance was very dangerous for all the firemen involved. It was a long night.

The next day, I was flying a training flight with two other pilots in the H-3. We made several practice IFR approaches, and touch and go landings to fulfill our flight requirements for the quarter.

On one approach toward the end of our flight, I was sitting in the flight engineer's jump seat just behind the pilot seats. I noticed a yellow caution light illuminate on the instrument panel. I reached up and tugged the instructor pilot's sleeve. He turned to look at me, and I just pointed to the panel.

"I have the aircraft," he said to the other pilot. He called the tower and told them we were terminating our flight due to mechanical problems. We pulled in and shut down the engines. Our crew chief got on board to find out why we came back early.

"We got a caution light on the main transmission," Maj. Robbins said. Sgt. Morse, our crew chief, climbed up and soon was back down and inside the chopper.

He held out his hand. "Sir, you guys came in at the right time. Look what is left of your main bearing," he said, nodding at the metal fragments in his hand.

If the caution light comes on, the aircraft flight manual instructs the pilot to pull and reset the circuit breaker to see if the light goes out. If not, you pull and reset the breaker a second time. If the light remains on, you need to land as soon as possible and check out the transmission. This time we were in the right place at the right time.

Later that evening, just before dark, a call came to all units from our base commander's duty officer. Someone had seen a guy in "black pajamas" climb over a remote fence, and he had a parcel in his grasp. Was he going to set off a bomb? Blow up some airplanes? Great!

Our 11 pilots, 7 engineers, and 16 PJs were gathered at the squadron. We had five H-3s, so our duty officer began to line up crews to go out and take off in case this guy was intent on blowing up our helicopters parked on the ramp. Somehow, using rank I guess, the pilots were paired off, with one pilot left behind to "be in charge"--me. The ground guys and PJs found some M-16s to pass out among those of us left at the detachment.

We watched the five H-3s taxi out and become airborne, and then monitored their radios. I then talked to the security police to get an update on the bad guy.

Suddenly, one of the NCOs came in and asked, "Sir, am I cleared to issue ammo to everyone?"

I thought a minute. It was dark and many people were moving about, mostly friends, and we all could look like a bad guy out there in the dark of night.

"Hell no," I said. "Let's make sure there *is* a bad guy out there before guns start blazing."

In a few minutes, a call came in from the security police. It was a false alarm. It is all clear. The five H-3s returned to base and landed. It was time to return the M-16s to their locked area. My night as "unit commander" was over, and all was well. 1970 was becoming a year to remember.

CHAPTER IX

RETURN TO UDORN-MARCH 1970

Spring arrived. There were more storms and heavy rains. Maj. Bob and I were called in to Lt. Col. Joe's office.

"Sit down," he said. "Your days in the H-3 at NKP are over. You are going back to Udorn tomorrow on the C-130 shuttle. You will be checked out in the H-53 and back in action soon. The remaining H-3 pilots are going to Da Nang, Vietnam, to join the 37th ARRSq and finish our tours there."

He got up, came over, and shook our hands. "You two pilots did a great job," he said. "Thanks for your efforts in doing our important work. God speed in the future."

That was the last time that I saw Lt. Col. Joe. I often wonder how his remaining days went. He was a great unit commander. He knew we had a tough job and how the daily potential for danger could affect us. He, too, flew many combat missions, so he knew exactly what we were up against. He didn't command his unit from behind a desk. He was a great leader and role model.

So, Maj. Bob and I once again packed up and got a ride to base operations to catch the C-130 shuttle. The only trouble was we were not going home, but back to Udorn Air Base and more war. Damn!

Back at Udorn, Maj. Bob returned to his old room and had to dig in to find his bed. He was always yelling at Capt. Ron about his mess. It was good fun and helped to break up any tensions that might develop doing this job. My roommate was Capt. Bill Furst. Usually, we were on different flight schedules, and it was rare if you flew in the same helicopter as your roommate. That was good, since he would most likely be the one who would pack up your things if something happened to you. That was something you thought about from time to time. I didn't have many personal items, just a few pictures, letters, and airline music tapes. Who would want my old socks and shirts?

It felt strange at first climbing back into the H-53 cockpit. It was larger, and it was nice to see the three six-barrel 7.62mm machine guns. Maj. Bob and I flew with one of the IPs to get re-qualified in the H-53. We both had enough combat time from our H-3 days to go into the aircraft commander upgrade program.

A normal day of flying "up north" from Udorn was this: Get up at 4 am and get on the crew bus by 4:40. Pick up your parachute, weapons, bulletproof helmet, and "blood chit," and then go to the morning briefing. That included the day's weather and, most importantly, our intel brief (usually by a young lieutenant who was in the intelligence field), which covered any downed aircraft and active rescue missions, if any. He also briefed us on the locations of all known anti-aircraft permanent sites and added comments on current mobile anti-aircraft weapons sightings. I circled all these with a black crayon so that, by looking at the map during the mission, I could sort out the best path to the objective while avoiding AAA sites. We did not want to fly over an AAA gun site--very bad for your health.

Then it was time to meet the other crewmembers. New guys were always showing up, and there were constant flight check-rides for the new crewmembers. Orientation, learning local procedures, was a bit more complex at Udorn since the base was much larger, and there were F-105s and T-28s flying from the base. Another group, Air America, also flew out of Udorn. They flew older fixed wing and helicopters. We knew they were CIA guys. You never saw much of them around the air base; it was like they were ghosts. They flew to strange places and often were shot down. Our rescue crews had saved a few of them, and they too saved a few of our fighter survivors.

They were also yanks, just in different flying suits. They knew we had their backs.

After our briefing, it was determined that we would fly up north, to Laotian General Vang Pao's headquarters. Once there, we shut down our engines and stayed on alert status in case someone was shot down in Laos or North Vietnam. We were an hour and a half closer to the action than if we were starting the mission from Udorn. That could make a difference in saving a downed pilot. Gen. Vang Pao was the leader of the Hmong people, and his army countered the North Vietnamese Army and other bad guys from Laos. Just prior to reaching his headquarters at Long Thien, Laos, we would rendezvous with an HC-130 and air refuel to top off our fuel tanks just prior to landing.

On the way north, after passing Vientiane, Laos, on our left side, there was a small remote area where the crews could check their mini-guns. It was one of the few times a pilot could get out of the seat and go back and pull the triggers. Engaging the left trigger would give an output of 2,000 rounds per minute. The right trigger increased the rate to 4,000 rounds per minute. Much more firepower than the M-60 guns on the H-3! People on the other end of these guns kept their heads down or got them blown off.

The landing area at Long Thien was a small landing strip running southeast to northwest. At the end of the runway was a very large rock. You might say it was their landing barrier.

Coming in, the crew looked for any other aircraft or helicopters. If clear, the landing was made into the wind. We then taxied to the east and parked. Once the engines were shut down, it was time to depart the H-53 and check out the immediate area. We set up our portable HF radio, with which we could establish contact with Air Force Headquarters in Saigon. They could then contact us in case we were needed to launch a search and rescue mission. One of the PJs stayed with the radio and maintained radio contact.

We had very few personal effects on our persons: our military ID card, a Geneva Convention Card, and our "blood chit". I was told to bring a few dollars to buy breakfast. We walked a short distance to a building where a rather hefty guy wearing an apron was frying bacon. He also had eggs in a bowl and potatoes on the grill. There was toast on a plate. The fee for this feast was a dollar. I figured the guy worked for the CIA, but I didn't ask. The place looked like a set from a John Wayne western.

We were always within a few minutes of our parked H-53. We did venture into what was a town. I noticed a dentist chair in the street as I walked along. A guy was seated there, and his legs were thrashing about. I guess the dentist didn't have any Novocain. A bit further down the street was a coin dealer with the latest book on U.S. coin values. Too much, I thought.

We had brought along some in-flight lunches. After lunch and clean up, we heard propeller aircraft in the distance--four T-28s flown by Laotian Air Force pilots. They made the tricky landing, turned off the runway, and taxied about 200 yards north of our location. Once parked, they begin to refuel and rearm. I noticed one of the aircraft had a pilot with a scarf flying out the cockpit.

"That is a Yank advisor," said Maj. Bert. "Our Yanks always taxi with a scarf hanging out." How did a Yank in his right mind get that job? Maybe he was a bit crazy.

Once the T-28s had shut down, the crew chief rolled out bombs, and another guy jumped up on the wing to refuel the aircraft while smoking a cigarette. We slowly got as far away from those guys as possible. When they finished, they closed up their cockpits and taxied out for departure. Off they went into the wild blue yonder. Good luck, T-28s. Good luck, Yank!

Before we left I made one purchase. The local jewelry dealer would make a silver bracelet with your name in gold for $25. There were also a tree and an elephant on either side of your name. Twenty-five bucks was a good deal for a silver bracelet. Minimum order was four for $100. Hopefully, we would be able to get back here in a month or two to pick up our goods. I think silver was a few bucks an ounce, and gold was $32 an ounce. I wondered if I should buy more of this Laotian gold . Maybe that would be a good retirement plan.

About an hour and a half before sunset, we started up the H-53s and left the site. Once airborne, I called the King HC-130 crew to give them our departure time and the area we would be flying, just in case we were needed for a search and rescue mission.

"King 3, Jolly 72 is airborne from channel 98."

"Roger, Jolly 72. Maintain this frequency."

There were many great sights to see in the mountains of Laos. Large waterfalls were plentiful in this part of the country. There were even secluded caves with monks peering out. How did they get way up there?

On our flight, Maj. Bob as lead jolly crew was a bit low and fast in his H-53 just ahead of us, and something was amiss. I looked out my window. A water buffalo was sprinting across a rice patty, frightened by the chopper. The water buffalo had a guy behind him with a harness wrapped around him, and he was not a happy camper. I called Maj. Bob on the radio, and he looked out and saw the problem. We pulled up and headed back to Udorn. Today was a quiet day. Tomorrow was another day, and who knew what might lie ahead. "Today was not my day to die" was a line I recalled from an old western.

CHAPTER X

NUMBER ONE HUNDRED-APRIL 1970

April 1970. It was time to fly with Maj. Prince and get my check ride as an aircraft commander in the H-53. Once certified, I would be totally responsible for four other lives. I needed to be able to assess each situation and make the proper decision. I knew that input from the other crewmen, the other pilot, the flight engineer, and the two PJs would be valuable. These guys knew what could get you in trouble.

As we came into the briefing room, I noticed a larger than normal group of people, both on the briefing stage and in the audience.

"Gentlemen," the briefer began, "this is a day from hell. There are over a dozen potential downed aircraft in Vietnam and Laos. We just got word of a C-130 gunship, call sign Dragon 34, that was hit at 10,000 feet. The aircraft exploded in the air. There are 13 crewmen on the aircraft, and we don't know how many got out."

Almost every helicopter from Udorn and Da Nang, South Vietnam, would be flying rescue missions today. Time for a check ride, and I get the real thing.

We flew eastward, crossing south of NKP and flying into Laos at 7,000 feet. Our Sandy A-1s joined up soon and checked in with us. The crew on the King HC-130 was busy assigning rescue aircraft as they checked in. We were assigned as "high bird" on the rescue mission for the downed C-130 gunship. It as getting late in the afternoon when, after a refueling, the on-scene Sandy Lead determined that only one crewman had safely parachuted from the C-130 gunship.

The other 12 never got out. They had taken a direct hit while flying at 10,000 feet and exploded.

Our "low-bird," Jolly 72, was having trouble with his radio transmissions, so I helped relay information to the King aircraft. Jolly 72 was able to get the C-130 crewman who had been thrown clear when the C-130 exploded. As Jolly 72 left the area, we joined up with him in formation.

"Jolly 72," came a call from our friends in the King aircraft. "Your flight has been directed to proceed to Da Nang to deliver the C-130 survivor and to remain overnight."

"By the way," he continued, "we were informed by higher headquarters that your pick up was number 100 for the 40th ARRSq. Congrats, guys. Sorry there were not more on this one."

In just a few years our squadron, the 40th ARRSq, had kept 100 crewmen from being killed or captured by the bad guys. It cost our squadron, though, as several of our guys had been killed or wounded. That is the high price of warfare. Some may die trying to save others.

I checked the map for the best route to DaNang. Our heading was 120 degrees, and we were 76 miles out. That would take about 35 minutes. Fuel status was OK. After a great landing, I taxied in and shut down our H-53 engines.

"Tom," said Maj. Prince, "you passed your check ride. You are now an aircraft commander in the H-53."

We checked in with our sister squadron, and they scrambled about trying to find empty beds. It turns out six of our H-53s were remaining overnight at Da Nang. That was about one-half of our squadron's helicopters. We knew many of the DaNang crewmen, since we had been through some of our training together. They had it a bit rougher than we did at Udorn. There was always a potential for "sapper attacks," so they kept blackout curtains on their windows.

The next morning, all six Udorn crews gathered for a briefing on our flight back to Udorn. Maj. Prince was our lead pilot, and I was flying as his co-pilot.

"Gentlemen," Maj. Prince announced, "we are all heading back in one large flight. In honor of our 100th rescue, we are Century Flight!" A big cheer went up.

As the six helicopters flew back to Udorn, one of our escort Sandy A-1s called us. "Century Lead, there is a 37 mm firing at you, and the last few helicopters in your flight have dispersed to avoid being hit."

We did not see any of the shells going off, since they were way behind us. Suddenly, one of the Sandy pilots came up on the radio.

"I have the bad guy in my sights."

I saw the A-1 pull up and then roll over and go into a dive.

"No more 37mm site," was a reply over FM radio.

"Thanks, Sandy Lead," we replied. "Let's go home, guys."

Wow, still four more months to go on my tour. Time here moves slowly, very slowly.

CHAPTER XI

WOMEN AND CHILDREN ONLY

Another month was put to rest. May 1970 arrived, and it was now closer to August. As an aircraft commander, I was more flexible for the guys in the squadron who made the daily flying schedule. It was almost like throwing darts at a board. Once most of the pilots were checked out, the schedulers could rotate us between flying as aircraft commander and co-pilot. We were mindful of who was "in charge" on each flight, whoever was designated the aircraft commander. You might be the aircraft commander on a flight as a captain, and your co-pilot could be a major or lieutenant colonel. The aircraft commander was the boss on that flight.

One day I was on the flight schedule flying as co-pilot for my roommate, Capt. Bill Furst. We were to fly on the north alert mission, and we were the primary Jolly or "low bird." Maj. Prince and Capt. Jim Blewitt were together in the high bird. The worst thing I remember about this time of my life was the "first lighter". That meant that you would be awakened by a very loud rap at the door followed by the feared expression: "Capt. Furst and Capt. Waldron, you have a first lighter. Bus pickup is in 30 minutes."

That day it happened. We were awakened at four am and given 30 minutes to get ready before pickup. First light was around 5:45 am. The bad guys were aware of our early missions, and they often would lie in wait to welcome us to the rescue attempt. We had a lot to do in a short time.

We grabbed all of our flight gear and weapons and had out our maps and notebooks ready to see where our mission location was. Looking around the room, I saw the

71

flight engineers and PJs in their seats, and eager to see where our crews were headed.

"Morning," said the major giving the briefing. He was a new guy, one I had not seen before. "Today, you Jolly Green crews have been given a special mission to fly up north near North Vietnam."

He continued, "I am the Operations Officer for the 20th SOS (Special Operations Squadron), and all of our H-3 helicopters are down for maintenance. We have none available to fly. There is an immediate need to evacuate many women and children from an outpost that is surrounded by North Vietnamese soldiers. The outpost is in far eastern Laos, and very near the border with North Vietnam. There are A-1s available to provide cover for your entry and exit from the area. You will proceed to Lima Site 98 (General Vang Pao's headquarters) and be given details of the exact pickup location and where you are to take the people. Are there any questions? If not, good luck."

The rest of our crew looked a bit puzzled by the day's mission. It was a mission unlike any that our Jolly Crews had flown in the past. The 20th Special Operation's crews were always off doing something sneaky with guys dressed in funny clothes. We never asked who their clients were or where they took them.

Prior to takeoff, our PJs and the flight engineer arranged our cabin area so we would have room for the evacuees. We started engines and taxied out for departure.

We flew north and passed Vientiane, Laos, off to our left. I called the King aircraft to set up an air refueling prior to our landing at Long Thein, Laos. We made a normal approach and landing at Lima 98 and shut down our H-53.

A jeep pulled up to take the Jolly pilots and PJs to the "CIA café". While we grabbed a quick cup of coffee, we were told someone was on the way to brief us on our mission. I heard an aircraft flying nearby, and then I saw a strange looking aircraft on final approach. It was a Pilatus Porter turboprop, a single engine aircraft and not a USAF aircraft.

The pilot hopped out of the Porter, jumped into a jeep, and came our way. He looked like a cowboy from Australia, with a big hat, large brown boots, and a 9 mm pistol on his hip. He pulled up to where we were, took out a map, opened it, and pointed at our location.

"Our location is here," he said. "You will head over there and land at the site." I quickly noted our destination. It was a small landing site, maybe ten miles from the border of North Vietnam.

"Once your passengers are loaded," he continued, "bring them back to this location." He jabbed his finger at a nearby Lima site on his map. "It is a safe area."

He started to return to his aircraft, but stopped. He turned around.

"Oh," he said, "I forgot; women and children only. No men are to get onboard your helicopters!"

I got with the other co-pilot, Capt. Jim Blewitt, and we determined what our compass headings would be to the landing site. We quickly determined how long it would take to get to the site and how much fuel we would use.

We drove back to our H-53s, strapped in, and started the engines. We were soon airborne, heading northeast toward our objective. We were in contact with our high bird using our FM radios. After twenty minutes of flying, I saw some white smoke.

I told Bill Furst, "Our landing zone is about five minutes ahead. We'll be turning right about ninety degrees and landing uphill, toward the south. It doesn't look like we will have much runway to use. I think we are going to find a lot of dirt and no asphalt there."

I heard the A-1 pilots talking on the radio, but I couldn't see them. They are using Hobo and Firefly call signs. I recognized a couple of their voices from previous rescue missions. They were placing bombs below the landing site. Damn, we were close to North Vietnam. Too close!

As we were making our final right turn to land, there were several bursts of mortar fire. Were they coming into the site, or were the good guys shooting them at the North Vietnamese troops? Bill and I couldn't tell if those rounds were incoming or outgoing. Our PJs were asking us to turn on the guns. They were antsy; hell, so was I. I decided to leave the gun switch off and turn it on before we departed.

I told the gunners in the back, "Hang on, guys. Let's make sure who the bad guys are before we start firing our mini-guns. I'll turn them on when we land so they are ready to use when we take off."

Many people surrounded the landing site. Most were sitting. We were the first Jolly crew to land, so they did not know how much blowing dust we would make as we landed and turned around. Bill had his hands full. We were both looking out for trees and other obstacles that might give us a problem. Meanwhile, the A-1s continued to come from our right and lay down 20 mm fire below the hill. There were bad guys below the hill, and those bastards would try to shoot us down when we left.

When we landed, Sgt. Fisk, one of our PJs, and our flight engineer, Sgt. Coburn, jumped down to help the women and kids get on board our H-53. Our other PJ, Sgt. Van Brunt, helped to sit them down from the rear forward. He had his hands full. None of us could speak their language, so the guys just pointed a lot.

I turned around and looked at the women and kids who were seated and looking straight ahead. I had never seen such a combination of fear and hope reflecting from faces before. They didn't know us, yet they had to trust that we would get them to safety. I don't know just how many people we had, maybe 30 or 40. The little kids were seated on their mom's laps. The men had to stay and fight. Then we were loaded and ready to go. "Bill," I said, "let me call Hobo 23 before we leave and have him lay down fire support as we takeoff."

"Do it," he replied.

"Hobo 23, Jolly 78 ready to depart with a full load and we will immediately turn west once we clear the site. Can you lay down some fire support from east to west?"

"Roger that," he said.

I saw the A-1 and his wingman begin their fire support run from the east. Damn, they were close to the North Vietnamese border! Our H-53 began a slow, but steady, takeoff roll. Both PJs and our flight engineer were on their mini-guns, ready to fire at the bad guys. The two A-1s laid down blazing gunfire aimed at the bad guys down the hill.

We just cleared the area, and I saw a lot of bullets pounding down below us. So far, we were OK and not taking any hits from enemy fire. I guess their heads were down--way down.

After flying twenty minutes, we found the safe landing site. We landed, and the PJs and flight engineer helped the women and kids get out. Someone was there to meet them. When the women and kids were unloaded, we took off and headed east to get more refugees. We passed our high bird, Jolly 79, coming in to discharge their passengers. Then we heard someone calling us over the UHF frequency.

"Jolly 78, this is King 1, over."

"This is Jolly 78," I said.

King 1 came back, "You are to return to base ASAP. Acknowledge."

"Roger that," I replied. We turned south and checked our fuel. It was OK.

After we landed, it was time to debrief with the special operations staff. We gave as much detail about the mission as we could remember.

Then, Maj. Prince spoke up. He looked at his engineer, TSgt. Montgomery, and said, "I am glad you were able to reach out and get that baby. I could see someone holding up a baby, and they were crying."

His PJ, TSgt. Hietsch, said, "When I took the baby into my hands and turned around, it was suddenly gone from my hands. It was passed back to its mom I guess."

Another PJ, Sgt. Hoberg, spoke up. Remember that guy in the big western hat with the 9 mm gun? He got on our H-53 and went back to a Laotian guy who had gotten on our 53. He pulled out his gun and pointed it at the guy's head. Then he pointed to the crew entry door. The guy moved to the door and out he went. Who *was* that guy in the big hat?"

Next day, since I had been to the rescue area, I was put on the schedule to fly with our operation's officer, Lt. Col. Frank Catlin. All went the same, and we made our way up north to our landing base in Laos to wait for our "cowboy" to return. But he never showed up. We got on the radio and called headquarters to see what was going on.

"Jolly 74, your mission has been cancelled," headquarters said. "No further attempts to rescue women and children are possible. Maintain your normal search and rescue mission plan for the day, over."

"Roger," I replied.

Damn, the place must have been overrun by the bad guys. How many women and kids got out? Did the soldiers get out? I guess we would never know what happened. Maybe someday I'll meet a kid who was on our chopper and ask him what happened after they made it to a safe area.

This war in South Vietnam had a big impact on the little country of Laos. The North Vietnamese soldiers would move men and supplies down and through several trails into Laos, and then into South Vietnam to use against our US Army soldiers and Marines. The US Navy and Air Force fighters and bombers could do a lot to disrupt those movements and keep the supplies out of the bad guys' hands.

We might never know just how much help we got from the people of Laos. I am sure it would be much more than they were given credit for. I don't think those many lives we saved that day in May 1970 were ever noted anywhere. No medals were awarded. But the crews who were there and those who got out would remember. So far, the bad guys had not made it to Thailand. People there were nervous; they thought they were next.

CHAPTER XII

LEROY IS GONE

Air Force crewmembers who fly combat missions are authorized a week of R and R (Rest and Recreation) during their tour. Since Maj. Bob and I had arrived in Thailand at the same time, we decided to fly to Hawaii where we could meet our spouses. It was great to put away everything military: flight suits, helmets, and guns. Only our shower-washed casual clothes went in the suitcase for the week.

When we arrived in Honolulu, the first thing I noticed was how my "clean clothes" had an odor unto themselves. I guess when you are around certain smells, your nose tells the brain to forget about it and live with it. The washing machines in Hawaii did a good job eliminating the odor.

After a very quick week of sand and cold beer and such, Bob and I headed down to Flight Operations Section on Hickam AFB to see if we could get a return flight (a hop) to Thailand. We were able to get on a C-141 that was to leave within a few hours. Our wives were headed back to the mainland on a TWA four-engine propeller aircraft, which would take awhile. Bob and I were going back to Thailand in a jet.

Bob and I made our farewells and headed over to Flight Operations to search out the C-141 crew who would give us a ride "home". It was early July 1970. The C-141 crew we were flying with was in the flight planning section. They had been in Thailand the previous week and, hearing that Bob and I were Jolly Green pilots, one of them asked: "Did you know the Air Force lost a Super Jolly Green?

"Are you sure it was an H-53?" we asked.

"Yes, it was an H-53. We don't have any details, but the crew was from the 40thARRSq."

Bob and I looked at each other with a strange feeling. We knew all of the pilots, engineers, and PJs. We tried to forget about it until we were back in Thailand. We could not do anything about it while flying in a C-141. Was Capt. Ron OK? How about my roomy Capt. Bill? Damn! It was like losing someone in your family. I guess they were our family, especially this year. They were all brothers.

The C-141 landed at Bangkok. Bob and I tried to find a phone to call our squadron to let them know we were back in country and would head back on the C-130 shuttle the next day.

"Who did we lose?" Maj. Bob asked.

The duty officer, Lt. Col. Shipman, told us, "Jolly 54 went down on a rescue mission for Nail 44, an OV-10 Forward Air Controller. They suspect a shoulder fired missile was used, and there were no survivors. It was Capt. Leroy Schaneberg's crew. See you guys tomorrow."

"Sir," Bob asked, "who was his co-pilot?"

"It was Maj. John Goeglein. The flight engineer was Sgt. Bell and the PJs were Sgt. Jenkins and Sgt. Dean."

Bob and I were in a state of shock. Five Jolly Green crewmembers were gone. We both had flown missions with each of them. Five souls were gone.

Jolly Green 54 would never fly again. Husbands, sons, dads, brothers, nephews, and friends were gone. Damn. Leroy's gone!

I first met Leroy Schaneberg in the mid-'60s when we were both in KC-135 squadrons. I was a young co-pilot and Leroy was a navigator. We were not on the same crew, but we would see each other while on alert in Indiana and Goose Bay, Labrador, Canada. I knew his wife, and he had a little girl. Leroy always wanted to be a pilot and applied for USAF pilot training, and he was selected. After Leroy completed pilot training, he and I again crossed paths when we were in the same H-3 and H-53 training classes. While reuniting and talking, we soon found out that both of us were going to Udorn Air Base to fly H-53s assigned to the 40th ARRSq.

Just before I headed off to Hawaii on my R andR trip, I had ventured down to Leroy's room. I went in to chat about what type of assignment we wanted after our combat tour. In less than six months, we'd be back home. Is it back to KC-135s, stay in H-53s, or head to graduate school? Leroy had a picture of his wife and little girl in an 8x10 picture frame. Leroy had bright red hair, which was rare.

That night Leroy and I sat around with our feet up, having a cold beer (beer only cost a dime at the BX). We talked about some of the old KC-135 guys back in Indiana and wondered where they had gone. Little did I know that when I said good night to Leroy that night, it was the last time he and I would ever speak?

I don't know who had the task of packing up Leroy's personal effects and sending them to his wife. I felt bad that I did not send along any kind of letter or card to his family. Maybe it's not too late to tell his family that Leroy was a great man; he put his life at risk to save others. He paid the ultimate price in giving his life. The same can be said of the other four crewmen--John, Marvin, Paul, and Michael. They were all heroes, and their memories should never die.

When I first arrived in Thailand, I remember seeing a cigarette lighter that someone had been given by an Army

Ranger friend. The lighter had a green emblem on one side and a verse printed on the back: "For those who fight for it, life has a special flavor the protected will never know."

Well, so long Leroy. You were a good friend. You will be missed. Since I became a member of the rescue family, twelve brothers had been killed in action. Gone, their lives snuffed out before they were grandfathers. And this tour is not over; still a few months to go.

CHAPTER XIII

BACK TO EGLIN AFB IN DESTIN, FLORIDA

On August 24, 1970, I turned the ripe old age of thirty one. With all that happened during the year, it seemed like I should be at least forty. Finally, re- assignment orders began to arrive for our group.

Since Maj. Bob and I had credit for one-half of our temporary duty time while flying in the KC-135s, we had nearly two months taken off our year's assignment. No complaints from us. Bob was going to a rescue squadron at Patrick AFB, Florida, which provided rescue mission support during space shuttle launches. Capt. Ron was headed to Hickam AFB in Hawaii flying the H-53s. I was going back to Eglin AFB in Florida to be an instructor pilot in H-53s. I would be the first fixed-wing conversion pilot to go back as an instructor in helicopters. So long KC-135s.

Our squadron usually had farewell/welcome parties so that the new crews could meet the "old ones" before they headed back to the USA. It was a bit tough saying adios to Bob and Ron. They still had a few more missions to fly and bullets to dodge. The night before I left was very quiet, since many of the guys had to fly combat missions the next day. I'd be going to Bangkok and boarding a Continental Airlines flight back to the west coast of the good old USA. Adios-SAMs, MIGs, and bad guys with other guns that liked to shoot at you. It should be relatively quiet in Florida, with only a few alligators to watch out for on the golf courses.

Destin, Florida, is on the Gulf coast, about 40 miles east of Pensacola. A few hurricanes had visited the area and blown down a few buildings and washed out roads. But the seafood was great. Shrimp, oysters, grouper, and red snapper were at the top of the menu. After getting the family moved from South Carolina and located in on-base housing, son David was enrolled in school. I was back in the grind, studying for my checkout as an instructor. I would be training new H-53 pilots to go into harm's way. What could I tell them that might keep them stay safe in the future and still do their mission?

My new boss was Lt. Col. Jack Allison. His boss was Lt. Col. Warner Britton, who was in charge of the three helicopter training units: the H-43 that provided local rescue and the H-3 and H-53 Jolly Green training units. The H-3 was being phased out, and the H-53 would be the future of USAF combat rescue for the 1970s. The HC-130s were also there so our pilots could get qualified in air refueling procedures.

Shortly after my arrival, I was called to Lt. Col. Britton's office for an awards ceremony. I was awarded the Distinguished Flying Cross for a mission I had flown as an aircraft commander on April 21, 1970, in the H-53. I was also awarded two more Air Medals, for a total of seven Air Medals. I now had Air Medals in three types of aircraft: KC-135, H-3, and H-53.

One of my new jobs was to schedule all of the training missions for the new H-53 pilots. I would coordinate with the C-130 group to schedule the required air refueling flights. The PJs "loved" the air refueling flights with new pilots on board. They got understandably nervous when new H-53 pilots and co-pilots were at the controls during their first air- refueling mission. Heck, so did I!

One morning, Lt. Col. Allison came into my area. "Tom, can you come into my office a second? Oh, and please close the door. Thanks."

So, I went in, closed the door, and had a seat.

"Tom, there has been a slight glitch in a special mission that we have been flying at night." (I remembered seeing several night flights involving only the instructors.) "Maj. Smith has developed a serious eye problem and will be grounded for quite awhile. I would like for you to volunteer to take his place flying with Maj. Donohue. I can't tell you where the objective is; it is highly classified since lives depend on secrecy. Please let me know tomorrow what your decision is. Thanks, that's all."

I got up and left the room to go home. It was going to be a long evening.

What was that all about, a secret mission? Where to? Cuba? Russia? China? Africa? With the H-53's ability to air refuel, it could go almost anywhere in the world. Great, I was just back from the war zone, and I couldn't say a word about this to my family or friends. How was I going to be able to pull this off without a glitch? I'd been gone for the last two Thanksgivings and Christmases, and they were just around the corner in 1970. But something inside me said, go for it.

The next day I went to Lt. Col. Allison's office. I knocked, entered his office, and gave my answer: "Colonel, I am on the team." I didn't know what was in my near future. Was I going back into the ring of fire? More MIGS and/or SAMs? More bad guys? Time would tell.

Later that day, Lt. Col. Allison took me over to Lt. Col. Britton's office, and I was introduced to several people in civilian clothes. I had no idea who those guys were. CIA? DIA? I remembered working with a guy with a 9 mm handgun a while back in Laos when we rescued a lot of women and kids. Secrecy seemed to be paramount.

My first night flight on the special mission was in late September 1970. Maj. Marty Donohue was flying as pilot, and I was flying as his co-pilot. Between us, we had a lot of helicopter flying experience. Marty had flown over 6,000 hours in helicopters, with more than a hundred missions in Southeast Asia, including a few into North Vietnam. Our flight engineer was SSgt. Aaron Hodges, and our two PJs were SSgt. Jim Rogers and SSgt. Angus Sowell III. Everyone on Marty's crew was an instructor in his position. All were combat veterans with a lot of combat hours, missions, and military decorations. There were no rookies on our crew. Lt. Col. Allison and Lt. Col. Britton were also involved. This was the first team. There were more flying hours in the H-53 with this small group than you would find anywhere else in the world. Maj. Jay Strayer from my old unit in Thailand was also there, flying as co-pilot for Lt. Col. Allison, and Maj. Al Montrem, another instructor pilot, was flying with Lt. Col. Britton.

We had a standard briefing to include weather and what was going on at Duke Field just north of Eglin AFB. Once we had landed at the range, Army Special Forces soldiers would climb on board with weapons. We would take off with them on the H-53, fly around, and then "attack" some sort of objective--a building with sheets attached. Was this a prison somewhere in Cuba? The Bay of Pigs fiasco was not that long before. Were some CIA guys being held prisoner there? Within our helicopter crews, there was a lot of speculation going on, and that was not good. The problem with a secret is that you could slip up talking to the right people in the wrong place. So we just kept quiet. I was convinced that our lives and the mission success depended on it. A lot of people knew that there was a lot of flying going on at Eglin AFB. Back in World War II, a group of guys did initial flight training at Eglin. Lt. Col. Jimmie Doolittle used the airfield to train his bomber pilots in short field takeoffs. They would later take off from a carrier in the Pacific in B-25s and bomb Japan. They even made a movie about that mission.

Our families began to wonder why we worked all day and also flew several late night flights a week. (We were not paid overtime in the military.) Wives often met and played cards and probably talked a lot. "Loose lips sink ships" is a saying from World War II that I had heard in many old movies. We could have added "and might shoot down helicopters."

The training flights became more intense as we added more helicopters and US Army guys. We would fly in formation with the C-130 and practice night air refueling with lights off. Maj. Donohue switched seats, since we were on the right side of the C-130, with two other H-53s on our left. He thought it provided a better line of sight looking out the left window rather than the right side, which was where the aircraft commander normally sat. He was correct. It was difficult to look toward the left at night with no lights. Some of our flights went up into Georgia, and when we returned for the assault, it was a little over three hours' flying time. We could leave from southern Florida and make it to Cuba and back in that time. That must be the target, I thought. Operation Ivory Coast was the code used for our missions. Were we going to Africa? Often I could see and hear the A-1s flying over the landing areas. I probably knew of few of the crews from NKP days. Sandy pilots and rescue usually went hand in hand. Where in the hell were we going?

Time became a factor. On a late October morning, all of the assault H-53 pilots--Lt. Col. Britton, Lt. Col. Allison,

Maj. Donohue, Maj. Montrem, Maj. Strayer, and I, and the two H-3 pilots, Lt. Col. Zehnder and Maj. Kalen, were driven to nearby Hurlburt Field, in Mary Ester, Florida. It was home of the USAF Special Operations Wing. We entered a large rectangular building, and saw the guys in civilian clothes that I had met a few weeks ago when I first joined this mission.

We went down a hallway and, our escort entered a special code on the door posted "Top Secret". We were then escorted inside a large briefing room. In the middle of the room was a big model, some four by five feet, sitting on wooden sawhorses. There was what looked like walls around what appeared to be some sort of camp. Inside were very realistic models of buildings and trees.

"Gentlemen," said the briefing officer, "meet 'Barbara'. That is the code name for your objective: a prisoner of war (POW) camp some 23 miles northwest of Hanoi. Operation Ivory Coast is the code name for the mission, a POW camp located outside of the small city of Son Tay, North Vietnam. We are going to fly there and bring back over 60 American Prisoners of War."

My jaw dropped. Hanoi was the area where SAMs and MIGs shot down most of our POWs. And now we would be headed there with US Army Special Forces to bring POWs home? Wow. Six helicopters flying in formation with a C-130 at night and no lights…

"Inside there are about 60 POWs from the USAF, USN, and Marines," the officer continued. "You are going to penetrate one of the most heavily guarded areas in the world. There are SAM sites, MIG airfields, and anti-aircraft artillery sites."

I looked around and saw the overall commander, Brig. Gen. Leroy Manor, commander of the USAF Special Operations Wing at Hurlburt Field. With him was a US Army Special Forces Officer, Col. Arthur "Bull" Simons, who was the ranking Army officer there. Wow, what a secret. I had never envisioned going back to where I had just flown in harm's way for the past year. I had not even thought about that possibility. Now, it was our objective-- Son Tay, North Vietnam. Just a few months earlier, I flew combat missions near the "lion's den," the North Vietnamese border. It was dangerous then, and soon we would be going inside the den itself.

I was now officially a member of the Son Tay Prisoner of War raiding team as an H-53 pilot. I was going back to that place we Jolly Green pilots called hell on earth: Hanoi, North Vietnam. Our Guardian Angels would once again be busy in the days to come, very busy.

CHAPTER XIV

FRUIT SALAD--THE SECRET IS OUT

After a short break to let the secret location soak into our heads, it was time for more briefings. Next up was Lt. Col. Ben Kraljev, one of Gen. Manor's staff. He began to give us his findings about the upcoming raid into North Vietnam.

"Many of our captured pilots and crewmen are dying in prison camps, mainly due to injuries not properly treated, malnutrition, and other health issues," he said. "Some of our aviators have been prisoners for over seven years. We need to send a message that, we, the USA, are concerned about the health and welfare of our soldiers in captivity. It has been decided at the highest level to proceed with this operation. (Did he mean President Nixon?) The question that has been asked by those in high places was what time of the month is best to attempt a rescue mission in North Vietnam?"

The briefing officer continued: "We know that your training sorties, which involve formation flying to include night air refueling without cockpit or external position lights, have been quite challenging. Our planning staff believes that with full moonlight conditions, your visibility while flying with the MC-130 will improve and help to identify the objective during the final leg of your attack. There are two future dates that meet the criteria: late October or November. This time of year there are threats of major cyclones in the area.

"As of now," he continued, "a final decision as to the launch date has not been made. You will be informed a few days prior to the date of launch. We will have C-141

Military Airlift Command aircraft at our disposal to move all of the men and equipment to Korat Air Base in Thailand, with fuel stops in California, Hawaii, Guam, and the Philippines. You will have temporary duty orders showing that you are on an inspection team, and there is a block checked on your orders that has "variations authorized" to cover our mission after it is over. Are there any questions? (I had a few, but I kept quiet.)

"The H-53 Jolly Greens assigned to the 40th ARRSq at Udorn Air Base will be available for us to use on the mission. The A-1s will be used from assets at Nakon Phanom Air Base (NKP), to the east of Udorn. Each A-1 will have an NKP pilot flying with the Hurlburt pilots."

It would be good to have the old Sandy pilots with us on the mission. Our cover story was that the H-53s had been grounded. Many flights were needed to test the perceived problem. Since we were all instructors, it would not be suspicious that we were going to Southeast Asia to help test the H-53.

Another of Gen. Manor's staff, Maj. Dick Pleshkin, got up to brief. He walked over to the POW camp model, Barbara. He pointed to the model and said "the camp is about 140 feet by 180 feet with walls that are ten feet tall and two feet thick." We analyzed our intelligence photos and saw two gun towers on the north and south sides of the western approach to the camp. We can assume there are guards with machine guns in each tower. As you go from west to east down the center of the camp, the buildings on the left side are our POWs' prison cells. The buildings at the center of the camp near the far eastern end are the prison camp commander's area. Special Forces will insert an assault team, called Blueboy, who will be flying in the

'Banana' helicopter, which will land in an open area inside of the camp. The assault team will go to each cell and release our POWs and then lead them to the southwestern wall for extraction and freedom. Oh, from now on the POWs are known as ' ITEMS'."

Maj. Pleshkin continued, "The joint planning staff came up with a unique diversion plan just prior to attacking the camp. The USN will be tasked to launch eighty plus jet fighters about 30 minutes before the assault team's arrival at the POW camp. That should keep the radar sites busy."

(President Johnson had created a no-bombing zone to include Hanoi back in October, 1968.) So, the North Vietnamese soldiers watching their radar scopes at two in the morning would wonder why are USN fighters, after a long period of not bombing Hanoi, attacking, and breaking President Johnson's pledge?

Great diversion! Our staff planners are using surprise and diversion-two great historical military options that have worked in the past. Hopefully, while watching some eighty fighters bearing down on Hanoi, the MIGs and SAMs would be looking East while the assault team (MC-130 plus six helicopters and one with five A-1s) slips in the back door in the west. Great plan, guys.

There were only a few US Army officers who knew where we were going. Most of the other soldiers would not know the target until the night of the attack. It was "need to know" only.

So why were we Air Force helicopter crews in the plan? I soon found out. Lt. Col. Britton stood and began to brief about what the Air Force Rescue helicopter crews would be doing on this mission. He had been involved from the beginning, which was great because he knew helicopters, particularly the H-53 model. Our H-53s were assigned call signs of Apple 1 through Apple 5. The fixed-wing A-1s were assigned call signs of Peach 1 through Peach 5. We had flown several training flights in formation with a US Army Huey, the H-1 helicopter, call sign Banana, which was to insert the Blueboy assault force in the compound. One of our MC-130s crew was from Germany, call sign Cherry 1. They would have the helicopters with them in formation. The other MC-130 and its crew were from North Carolina, and they had the Air Force A-1s flying formation on their wings; their call sign was Cherry 2.

When the Army H-1 flew in formation with the H-53s and the MC-130, the airspeed was well below 100 knots and required a complex drafting procedure on its part. The H-3s and H-53s could easily fly at 125 to 135 knots and not give the HC or MC-130s any control problems. Our Army ground commanders began to sense something was not right. The H-1 could only fly for a couple of hours and then needed fuel. The H-1 could not be refueled from the air, so they would have to land somewhere in Laos or North Vietnam for fuel. Not a good idea. The Huey had another limitation in that it could only carry 11 of the Blueboy attack element, versus 14 if an H-3 was used. Another plus for using the USAF H-3 was the fact that it could be air refueled while flying in formation the same time the H-53s were air refueling. Also, the higher airspeeds of the H-3 and the H-53s were compatible, allowing the MC-130's helicopter formation to arrive at the camp much sooner.

I felt badly for the Huey pilots, as they would now a have backup role. Several issues still remained, and we continued to examine each detail of the mission. With all of the talent involved, we knew solutions would be found. All of the H-53 pilots and crewmembers were combat experienced and were instructors in their individual specialties. This was the first team.

Then, Colonel "Bull" Simons stood and began to express his main concern about the very beginning of the assault. Since the Army H-1 Banana helicopter was not going to be used, with its experienced Army gunners, how could the two gun towers be neutralized as we inserted Blueboy Force (now inside the H-3 USAF helicopter) into the compound? We couldn't risk landing inside the camp if there were gunners in the towers who could take out our Blueboy assault force. The USAF H-3 would have a tough time landing inside the compound with the trees and buildings close by. Could they also take out the gun towers prior to landing? Maybe it could be done.

As mentioned earlier, the H-3 had less fuel than the H-53 and had to jettison external tip tanks prior to possible small arms fire to avoid an explosion if hit by a bullet. (I had to jettison H-3 fuel tip tanks a few months before, when we went in to pick up a downed USN pilot.) The fuel status of the H-3 would then be down to less than an hour's flying time, and that was not enough to reach a C-130 tanker in a safe area to air refuel. It was also very likely the H-3 could be damaged when making the confined landing. So, the assumption was it would not be coming back. A decision was made to blow up the H-3 using a timing device set to go off 10-15 minutes after the last H-53 loaded with our ITEMS departed the POW camp. The three Air Force crewmen in Banana and the 14 Army Special Forces, Blueboy element, would get into Apple 1 or Apple 2.

Standing up, Lt. Col. Britton explained. "Apples 3, 4, and 5 will be called in to load up our ITEMS. A little over twenty plus ITEMS and off you go. The PJs will examine each ITEM en route, and provide any life-saving medical attention needed. The Army will have prepositioned water and baby food. Lt. Col. Cataldo, an Army surgeon who will be on the mission, has dictated that these items be on each of our H-53 choppers. There will also be blankets and slippers. The additional weight should be negligible. We can assume the ITEMS may also be in shock. They may experience joy and want to stop and give you a big hug. We will have to do that after we land in Udorn. There will be a medical evacuation C-141 aircraft at Udorn that will transport the ITEMS back to Hickam AFB in Hawaii for medical attention as required."

The USAF elements would have specific tasks. The H-3, Banana 1, would land inside the compound with the 14 Army soldiers (Blueboy). They would go to each prisoner's cell and cut off the locks with bolt cutters. Then, they would bring out the prisoners and lead them to the southwest corner of the camp for extraction. The other assault H-53s, Apple 1 and Apple 2, would have the remaining 42 Special Forces soldiers in two elements, Redwine element and Greenleaf element.

Lt. Col. Britton would be in the lead H-53, Apple 1. On board would be Army Special Forces Col. "Bull" Simons (personal call sign Wildroot) and his force, the Greenleaf element, a total of 22 men in this support group. The remaining 20-man force would be on Apple 2, flown by Lt. Col. Allison with his USAF crew. Lt. Col. Sydnor was ground force commander of the US Army attack forces at Son Tay; his force was known as the Redwine element.

Col. Simons then stood up and repeated his concern. "I have more than a 100 volunteers for this mission. My officers have begun to reduce our team from 108 volunteers down to our mission total of 56. This is no easy task. All of these men are highly experienced, and I would trust any of them with my life. I still feel something needs to be done so that I can be sure that those two gun towers will not take out our Blueboy element landing inside the compound. I realize that using our Army Huey H-1 as a gunship, with all of its limitations, is not feasible because of lack of fuel and weight limits. Do any of you have any other suggestions?"

Then, the future mission of Apple 3 in this assault plan suddenly changed. To my left, Maj. Marty Donohue stood up and addressed Col. Simons. "Sir, I am Maj. Marty Donohue, Apple 3 aircraft commander. In addition to taking out our ITEMS, Apple 3 can first complete the task as mission gunship and make sure the way is clear for Banana to land without enemy machine gun fire from the two towers on the west end of the compound."

"Go on," said an encouraged Col. Simons.

"On our final approach to the camp," Marty said, "say some 10 miles west of Barbara, our helicopter can drop down from our formation position and take over as formation lead for the last three or four miles, with Banana and Apples 1 and 2 behind us in trail formation on our right side. Apples 4 and 5 have the backup flare mission, so they would stay with Cherry 1. We can find the POW camp after the four flares are deployed from Cherry 1. We can line up near the center of the camp and continue to fly at forty feet altitude and airspeed under twenty knots. My gunners on the left side and right side can fire our mini-guns and take out the gun towers. We also have another mini-gun on the rear ramp that could take out any other potential targets. Sir, these mini-guns can fire up to 4,000 rounds per minute.

"With Apple 3 taking out the two gun towers," Marty continued, "that would leave the landing assault area inside the compound clear from hostile fire from the towers and allow the Banana H-3 with the Blueboy element to land inside the compound without hostile gunfire from the tower. Apple 3 would then turn about 180 degrees and land a mile back from the camp, adjacent to where Apple 1 and Apple 2 will be landing after inserting their Army attack forces. Apple 3 would then revert to our mission of extracting ITEMS from the camp." Marty had thought this plan over, and it made sense to me.

Col. Simons looked at Marty and said, "Major, I am from Missouri, so show me." He looked at the staff and said, "I want Apple 3 to do a test flight to see if the crew can handle this gunship mission. If there is just one bullet hole in the area of the ITEMS, it is off. Good luck!"

I knew our three crewmen in the back were among the best in the USAF on the mini- guns. It was like challenging Matt Dillon, Paladin, and Wyatt Earp to a gunfight!

The briefing concluded with details about how the MC-130 would drop several flares over the POW Camp with Apples 4 and 5 serving as backups. Those two H-53 crews would need more training, since neither had performed that mission in the past.

Then we were told how the MC-130 would drop a "combat package" several miles to the south of the camp. That would delay any enemy troops heading our way. The planners had thought of several great diversions with this and the USN fighter diversion. This was a great joint, team effort with all services involved.

From my recent experience, I knew that flying into North Vietnam at night, with six helicopters flying on the wing of an MC-130 (no external or internal lights), would be very challenging with all of the SAM sites, MIG airfields, and radar sites along the way.

We would need F-105's to take out SAM sites, if needed, and F-4s or F-105s configured with air to air armament to take on any MIGs that might be launched.

Security continues to be important. If the bad guys knew we were coming, a lot of C-130s' A-1s and helicopters would be sitting ducks!

As Apple 3, we'd be the last H-53 into the camp to load up rescued prisoners (ITEMS), and any Army soldiers that would be there. The other H-53s, Apple 4 and Apple 5, were being flown by pilots on loan from Thailand and South Vietnam. (They had been in Florida all this time to train with us as a group.) They were to hold in an area five miles west of the Son Tay camp at a place called Finger Lake. The US Army ground commander would call them in, one at a time, to load up ITEMS. No one would be left behind. Our next challenge was to see if we could become the gunship for this mission. We left Hurlburt Field and returned to Eglin to plan our next mission. We also had our current students to contend with, and that had to continue. It was busy times for flyboys at Eglin AFB.

Maj. Pleshkin had given the attack group--MC-130s, H-3s, H-53s, and A-1s, all with call signs with names of fruits. Thus the nickname "fruit salad" was invented for our group. Our last fruit item was Lime 1, which was a King C-130 that would air refuel us after takeoff and before attacking Son Tay. So, Lime, Cherry, Banana, Apple and Peach were our call signs--one big fruit salad, and, an Air

Force rescue crew had become an Army assault gunship--
Apple 3.

The Russian satellites' schedules would dictate our
training mission time to fire the mini guns on Apple 3.
Could our USAF crew qualify as a gunship for this
important role of taking out the gun towers? The planners
did not want the Russians to see an H-53 flying around in a
rectangular pattern, trying not to hit large white sheets
attached to wooden frames. The planners did not want to
take a chance on giving any information away. Two days
later, about 1400 hours (2 pm), our Apple 3 crew launched
and headed to the gunnery range outside of Hurlburt Field.
This was a bit strange, since on this gunnery mission we
were trying to hit something (gun towers), while trying to
miss something else, the large white sheets that represented
the POW cells.

The planners had assembled a mockup that replicated
the two gun towers on the gunnery range, with clean white
sheets attached to wooden planks down the left side of
center where the ITEMS would be housed. Col. Simons had
said earlier that if one bullet hole was in a sheet, it was a no
go. Around we went, Maj. Donohue and I taking turns flying
at forty feet and twenty knots down the center of the model
compound with our PJs (Rogers and Sowell) and our
engineer, SSgt. Hodges, taking turns firing the mini- guns
from all positions. We also had Col. Simons and a couple of
his officers on board. They had not used the six-barrel min-
guns at 2,000-4,000 rounds per minute. It was a bit noisy
back there.

We flew for an hour and a half, and then it was back
to Eglin AFB to debrief. There was a large white sheet
folded in the front of the room. Our crew was as curious

about our results, as were the Army officers present. Col. Simon came in, cigar in hand, and sat down in the rear of room. (Simon reminded me of John Wayne. I was glad he was on our side.)

Col. Simon nodded to the briefing officer, who then got up and began. "Col. Simon, gentlemen, we removed the sheets from the camp model and examined each panel. Sir, we found no evidence of any bullets striking any of the cloth sheets. Therefore, we recommend that Apple 3 be designated as gunship for the Son Tay mission."

Col. Simon stood up and said, "Do it," then turned and left the room. He was a man of few words.

So there I was, ready again to go into harm's way. But, once again I was surrounded by heroes: Air Force Rescue crewmembers, Army Special Forces- Green Berets. It does not get any better than that! We would be fulfilling the role of attack gunship for the US Army elements. Apple 3 would have a dual role-- first into the assault area as gunship, and then last out with POWS and any other US forces still there. Marty and I discussed the mission and agreed no one would be left behind-not on our watch!

There seemed to be a lot of knowledge as to the number of POWs imprisoned at Son Tay. Estimates of between 61 and 65 POWs were mentioned at several briefings. We had three H-53s, and each could get 25 to 35 on board. Was there a spy inside Son Tay? How did we know that three H-53s would be enough? Alot of us had friends who were being held prisoner in North Vietnam. Were they at Son Tay?

Until it is time to go, we'll just keep doing our jobs, and wait for the signal to pack up for a TDY trip as an

inspection team to Thailand, "with variations authorized."
My guardian angels were back in business.

CHAPTER XV

THE TIME IS NOW

October 1970 passed without our being launched, so the next window of opportunity would be later in November. Thanksgiving was Thursday, November 26. I could not discuss with the family what we would do-- maybe go to the Officer's Club, so then there would be no need to cook. That was a good option. It was Friday, the 13th of November. The morning training flights for our new H-53 students would be complete by noon. After the students left, Lt. Col. Allison came into the instructors' area and said, "We have a meeting in Lt. Col. Britton's office- NOW!"

I guessed the time had come. The Apple crews and the Banana crew assembled in a secure area, and Lt. Col. Britton came in and closed the door.

"As you might of heard," he said, "the H-53s are grounded world-wide, so that means our inspection team will leave Hurlburt Field this Sunday night. You'll be picked up in front of your quarters at 1930 hours. Have your personal and flight gear packed and ready to go. Your Temporary Duty orders will be activated Sunday morning. Tell your family that where you are going does not have communication capability to make personal calls, so you will be isolated for a short time. Hopefully, we will be back for Thanksgiving. With the H-53s grounded by the Pentagon edict, our students should not wonder where we are, since they will be off for a few days and won't be at the squadron. Good luck, and God speed."

Sunday evening came rather quickly. I made my farewells to my wife and boys. I took my personal and flight gear in hand and walked to the curb to wait for the shuttle to pick me up. I looked around and wondered. Will I be back for Thanksgiving in a few days or be a new resident in a POW cell? Or? No time to think about that! I had to be on top of what was about to happen. I was going back to Udorn Air Base, Thailand. I just left there a few months ago. They even gave me a farewell gift and a party.

Among the five Apple crews were two Udorn H-53 pilots who had been flying the training flights with us, Maj. Ken Murphy and Capt. Bill McGeorge. I knew both of them while I was at Udorn earlier in the year. Bill and I were the only two USAF captains flying in the helicopter assault/rescue group; the rest were majors or lieutenant colonels with many combat hours and years of flying experience. All of the team-- pilots, engineers, and PJs--were combat tested veterans. The Air Force was sending in the first team to go with the Army's 56 highly trained, combat experienced, Special Forces soldiers.

One by one the Eglin aircrews checked in and got boarding passes and box lunches. One of the Eglin fixed-wing pilots with us was Maj. Bill Kornitzer, Jr. He was an HC-130 instructor pilot at Eglin and would fly as aircraft commander with a flight crew presently stationed in Thailand. Their mission call sign was Lime 1. They would provide the air-refueling platform for the H-3 and H-53s. We were glad to have them close by.

Military Airlift Command (MAC) provided C-141s to transport the aircrews and Army unit to Thailand. From Florida, we stopped at Travis AFB, California, changed the C-141 aircrew, and refueled. Then on to Hawaii to land, refuel, and change flight crews again. We had already logged over 11 hours flying time and a few hours on the ground. Then, we flew to Guam, Philippines, and, finally,

Tahkli Air Base, Thailand, some 28 hours later. We still had a few days to review flight plans and mission operational procedures before Sunday's proposed attack. After checking into quarters, we changed into our khaki uniforms so we wouldn't look like many aviators in flight suits wandering about the base with no airplanes to fly.

The Air Force crews, Apples, Banana, Cherries Limes and Peaches, all assembled in a secure room for briefings on the Son Tay mission plan, and the all-important weather forecast. The intelligence officer reported that recent pictures taken from the air showed activity inside the compound of "Barbara". I would never ask what method was used; that way, if I was captured, I could not tell anything.

The flight crews updated our flight maps to plot current known AAA sites, SAM sites, and MIG airfields. Nothing changed--still lots of bad guys with guns of all types. The place where we were going (near Hanoi, North Vietnam) was circled by many big guns, and a whole lot of bad guys. Our projected launch was this Saturday evening in order to hit the Son Tay camp around 0215 local time on the morning of November 22. While we were firing our mini guns at the guard towers at Son Tay, American sports fans would be watching college football on a Saturday afternoon. I wondered who the Clemson Tigers were playing.

The weather officer was the next to brief. "Gen. Manor, Col. Simon, we may have a weather problem for the November 22 timing," he said. "As you know, Cyclone Patsy is moving in from the east. At 0200 on the 22nd, we expect low visibility, very heavy rains, and high winds in the Son Tay area, which will cause extreme hardship for the assault on the camp. Sir, we recommend you move the date forward at least 24 hours, or delay launch for at least a week."

I noticed a few heads moving about and words exchanged. Then, Gen. Manor stopped the briefing, got up, and left the room with Col. Simon and a few planners. I assumed they had a long distance call to make on a secure line. If our launch were moved up a day, then the launch would be Friday evening, the 20th, in order to arrive at Son Tay the following morning, around 2 am. Time was suddenly being compressed.

With the local time change of plus twelve hours compared to Florida, it was not easy getting my body clock adjusted. I knew I needed to be rested. With a late night takeoff and early morning assault, I was going to need a lot of adrenaline--and soon. As we got back to our quarters to get some sleep, Gen. Manor and his planners were talking to those in high places. Many launch times needed to be changed for many different units, most of whom did not have a clue as to why they were to fly late at night and for what. They and the rest of the world would soon find out.

On the 19th, we were notified that we are back on. The launch was set for the evening of November 20, with the assault to be around 0215 local time in North Vietnam in the early hours of the 21st. I had not brought many personal items with me. My billfold had a few pictures and my driver's license that I was leaving behind in the desk drawer. In a pocket of my flight suit were my Military ID card, a Geneva Convention card, and, soon, a "blood chit".

Before we went over to the briefing room for our final briefing, I cornered Maj. Bill Kornitzer, my roommate in Tahkli. "Bill, I am leaving my billfold here in this desk, just in case something happens. I don't want to give the bad guys any more information than needed." Bill nodded, and I was off to war again.

It was a short walk over to the briefing room. The big difference was that the Army Green Berets were all there. They were in combat uniforms, and I was glad they were on our side! Most still did not know where the target was. The ranking Army officer, Col. Simon, came up to the stage, and the whole group, Army and Air Force crewmen, stood at attention.

"Seats!" was the command from Col. Simon. "The US assault forces are here and will soon be departing: Redwine, Greenleaf, Blueboy, and the Apples, Peaches, Banana, Cherry and Lime crews."

He continued, "I know you want to know where we are going tonight. After several months of intense training, early this Saturday morning it will be complete. Gentlemen, we are going to attack a North Vietnamese prisoner of war camp some 23 miles northwest of Hanoi, just outside the village of Son Tay. We are bringing home 61 US Prisoners of War to have Thanksgiving dinner in freedom with their families."

The Green Berets were on their feet, fists pumping, with many loud hoorahs. The adrenalin was all ready flowing. Those brave men trusted the Air Force Rescue crews, A-1 fighters, and the C-130 combat aircraft escorting the helicopters and A-1s into the heart of North Vietnam. They trusted the Air Force crews to get them there to do their jobs, and then get them back home in one piece. Having that trust was a great honor.

The room quieted down a bit and the briefing continued. Weather in the area was soon to worsen. Cyclone Patsy was closer to our assault area, and the surface winds going at the target area would be very strong from the north, or coming from our left. This meant the attack force would drift to the right without proper drift heading correction. The lead MC-130 navigator in Cherry 1 would announce a corrected heading to the assault formation over the radio at a point about 11 miles west of the camp.

Marty turned to me and said, "Tom, I am going to add another five degrees to the left of the heading the C-130 navigator gives us. I 'd rather be a bit north of the camp than south."

"Roger that," I said. "We'll add five degrees left."

I had gone over the target area many times. I could see where the POW camp was just west of the village. A river, just west of the camp, ran from the northeast to the southwest of the camp. About a quarter mile south of the camp was a facility called "secondary school". It was located inland from the river and near a fork in the roads. I did not have any other info on that place.

It was time to go. One by one we departed the briefing facility. I walked to the nearby hanger on a raised wooden sidewalk which keeps you from stepping on a cobra. Before reaching the hanger, I stopped and looked behind me. No one was there. No one was ahead of me. I was there all alone. I jogged the last few yards and entered the hanger which had several crewmembers all ready loaded onto the bus. The bus would take us to a transport C- 130 parked on the ramp, then, on to Udorn to get into our H-53s. The time is now.

CHAPTER XVI

OFF WE GO

Our C-130 transport departed at 2000 hours from Tahkli Air Base, landed at Udorn before 2100 hours, and parked on their ramp. The USAF helicopter crews got onto a crew bus that took us to the H-53 squadron's operations area. It was strange to look out my window and see a building I had entered many times in the recent past. As I walked toward the entry steps, I looked left and saw our H-53s all in a line from north to south, with the H-3 parked in the row behind. The five H-53s were for our Apple crews, and the H-3 was for the Banana crew. I also noted what appeared to be mission spares; two more H-53s and another H-3 parked one row behind the others. If one of the Apples had mechanical problems, the crew would need to get over to the spare H-53 ASAP.

If I had still been stationed there, I would have wondered why all of those H-53s and H-3s were out there ready to fly somewhere, when no one in the 40th squadron was tasked to fly. And just a few days before, the Air Force grounded the entire H-53 fleet. What is going on? As I looked into the window, I saw a few pilots I knew.

Lt. Col. Ed Modica, the 40th ARRSq commander, had arrived in March of 1970, just a few months before I departed for the USA. I wondered what he was thinking when tasked to have all of those helicopters ready to go for a 2300 takeoff time that evening, with none of his crews tasked to fly them.

The door opened and the parade of H-53 crewmembers, mostly from ARRTC, began. Lt. Col. Modica's jaw dropped. In walked several senior pilots that

109

he knew from his recent Eglin AFB training. In addition to Lt. Col. Britton, Lt. Col. Allison, and Lt. Col. Zehnder, there were Lt. Col. Royal Brown from Da Nang and several majors from ARRTC, as well as two of his pilots who had been on temporary duty at Eglin AFB, Maj. Jay Strayer , and Capt. Bill McGeorge. I was tagging along in the rear, and I saw Lt. Col. Modica give me a "what in the hell are you doing back here" look.

"Col. Modica, good to see you, sir," I said, taking his right hand in mine and giving it a good shake. "I'm back."

Just then, the squadron staff duty officer, Capt. Rich Baskett, who had attended my farewell party, came up to me and mumbled, "Why the hell are you back at Udorn? Where are all of you headed in our Jolly Greens?"

"Rich," I said, "I can't say. You'll have to watch Armed Forces TV tomorrow." The secret was still in play!

I gathered my weapons, a .38 caliber pistol, and an M-16 rifle; then, my parachute, and my "blood chit". I loaded my .38 and placed it in my holster above my heart, along with a few more rounds in the vest. I had time for a quick visit to the men's room. Then, pack up my gear for the walk down the steps and along the ramp to find Apple 3. The time had come.

One by one, the aircrews exited the operations building and looked for their assigned H-53s. The helicopter ground crews scampered around each helicopter to insure they were ready for flight. I counted back from the north and saw the third H-53. Not a Jolly Green call sign this evening, this H-53 was now Apple 3, the mission gunship. We are first over the POW camp at low altitude, less than 40 feet. Our three gunners were ready. I hoped the North Vietnamese gunners would be sound asleep at two am. All of this training, and coming a long distance for a few seconds over the POW camp! Only a few seconds to take out the two enemy tower gunners in order to protect our Banana helicopter landing inside the POW camp with the fourteen man , Army Blueboy element.

I went inside our H-53 and put my gear in the right seat for this mission. As instructor pilots, we often flew in either seat, depending on our student category, i.e., a new co-pilot or aircraft commander. Marty had chosen to fly this mission in the left seat, normally the co-pilot's position in a helicopter. With all external and internal cockpit lights turned off for this mission, he felt his visibility while flying formation with other H-53s was much better from the left seat. Based on recent night training flights, I agreed. My vision from the right seat looking across the cockpit at night without lights for reference was very difficult. Regardless of which seat he was in, Maj. Marty Donohue was the "boss" on this mission.

As in the past, each H-53 pilot's M-16, with an ammo clip inserted, was hung over the top of the opposite pilot's seat. (Yes, the safety was on.) I also had a bandoleer of M-16 ammunition hanging over the top part of the seat. You could never have too many bullets!

"Tom, go ahead and do the outside pre-flight," Marty said.

"Roger," I replied.

I grabbed my small flashlight and stepped back down on the ramp. I walked around the outside of our H-53, looking under the helicopter to check for any hydraulic or fuel leaks and found none. I stopped and look upward. Many stars were out that night. To my left, I saw many people milling about outside each helicopter. The Army elements were putting their gear on Apples 1 and 2, just next to us. After the pre-flight was completed, it was time to get back inside and strap in.

Our three crewmen were in the fuselage area behind the pilots' seats checking out their mini-guns. PJ Sgt. Jim Rogers was on mini-gun number one, which was out the left window. His target would be the north tower of the POW camp. Flight Engineer (FE) Sgt. Paul Hodges was on the number two mini- gun, which swings out into the crew entry door opening. Paul's target would be the south gun tower, on my side of the helicopter. PJ Sgt. Angus Sowell III (Wally) was our backup on an M-60 machine gun in case a forward mini-gun jammed. If both forward guns fired, he could lay the M-60 down and run back to his ramp gun to cover our rear. These guys were beyond good. They knew their way around the H-53; they knew just what was expected of them during this mission. I was honored to fly with them.

During combat rescue missions, there was another piece of personal equipment used by the pilots that was not used in stateside training flights. This equipment was a bulletproof ceramic vest. It fit under the pilot's shoulder straps, and it was supposed to protect your heart from a direct hit from small-arms fire or flying shrapnel from an explosive burst. Marty and I each had one lying there in our seats. Before strapping into my seat, I did a final walk about the cabin area with the two PJs. We had special items on board just for our POWs: bottled water, jars of baby food, slippers, and blankets. The Army doctor on the mission, Lt. Col. Joseph Cataldo, who was with the assault Redwine element, deemed these items necessary. It was great to have a doc along.

I looked out our rear ramp with its mini-gun bolted down, and just behind us I saw the Blueboy element, all 14 soldiers, getting into Banana, the H-3. Since the H-3 was not to return, the three Air Force crewmen would have to join the Blueboy element to get a ride home on one of the Apple H-53s. There were no PJs on Banana, just two pilots and a flight engineer. With 14 Army guys inside, I was sure they could find a couple to man the two M-60s on board. They were the backup gunners to take out the gun towers in case we were blown away.

Marty and I strapped in and began the pre- engine start checklist, when PJ Jim Rogers came on the interphone.

"Sir, what do we do with these Claymore mines?" he asked.

"What Claymore mines?" I said.

"Well," Jim said, "one of the Army guys just handed me these two Claymore mines and said if we go down they can set up a perimeter defense with them."

I turned to Marty. "Sir, what do you know about some Claymore mines the Army left on our doorstep?"

Marty looked at me and said, "What Claymore mines?"

I replied, "Our PJs say one of the Army guys just dropped off a couple of them."

Marty went on the FM limited range radio and asked Lt. Col. Britton the same question. No one seemed to know why Claymore mines suddenly appeared at Apple3's doorstep. I thought the Army just liked to pull off surprises. Well, it worked. I turned and asked Jim Rogers, "If a bullet hits one of the mines, will it explode?"

No one seemed to know if they would or not. I made a quick decision.

"Marty, Sir, give me your chest protector!" He looked puzzled. I said, "The PJs can put both of our vests around the Claymores. If a stray bullet comes through the cabin, the vests might keep them from exploding." (So much for our chest protection.) Before I work with the Army again, I told myself, I'd read up on Claymore mines.

We were about to do something that I had never done before: start engines, taxi, takeoff, and depart an airfield, all without getting verbal clearance from ground control, the control tower, or departure control. A green light illuminating from the Udorn Control Tower would be Apple 1's signal to taxi. We all will follow him and line up for takeoff. No talking. Six helicopters and three C-130s would be doing a silent departure from Udorn. Five A-1s would likewise do a silent departure at NKP.

Then, I heard the C-130s running up. The JP-4 fumes were thicker. A member of Gen. Manor's staff was in the Udorn Air Base control tower. Another staff officer was in the NKP control tower some 100 miles east, where the A-1s would also soon depart. A little after 2305 (11:05 pm local), we started both engines. I could just make out a C-130 rolling down the runway heading eastward. The mission was on.

The late night air was still and full of JP-4 exhaust fumes from the six helicopters that were still parked. The winds were calm. The great news was none of the assault helicopter crews required a spare helicopter. We waited for our green light for taxi/takeoff. There it was: Green Light. It was 2315 hours (11:15 pm). Like we were reading each other's minds, the three H-53s taxied behind each other and went to the end of the taxiway. Then it was time to add power and pull into a hover. Our interior lights were not on, so I leaned forward to check the engine instrument readings, and they were all in the green. On our left, Apple 1 began his departure, followed by Apple 2, and then we were off-departure time-2317.

We flew directly across the active runway. Next stop: Son Tay POW Camp, North Vietnam. All internal and external lights were still off, and radios were quiet. Taking off behind us were the Banana-(H-3), and Apples 4 and 5. They would be on the left side of our formation with the C-130s.

We slowly began to gain altitude. Our projected time to the POW camp was about three hours, which would get us there at 0215 on the morning of November 21. That was way past my normal bedtime, but not tonight.

Suddenly, radio silence was broken. Someone called out a "Break" command, which was used only in case of a possible collision. We turned 30 degrees right and climbed 500 feet as we had done during training. After 30 seconds, we returned to our original heading. I thought I saw some red/green lights flash nearby, just below the formation. They had to come from an aircraft that was not part of our group. Who was flying that airplane? The CIA? The Thai Air Force? What a way to start. Then, the intruder aircraft was gone. We got back into our proper positions and began to look for the HC-130, Lime 1.

The moon was rising, but it was still low on the horizon to the northeast. The moonlight would greatly improve our ability to see the HC-130, Lime 1,who was moving over from our left. He was level at3000 feet. All five of the H-53 Apples and the Banana H-3 slid into their proper formation positions. The HC-130, our "mother hen," now had her six chicks on her wings, three on each side. I leaned forward so I could monitor the various readings on our instrument panel, including our fuel consumption. Marty was totally focused on the other two H-53s on our left and keeping us in position.

Our flight plan took us directly north over a TACAN station, code name Skyline, Channel 108 on our instruments. I had used this site to navigate in the past while flying rescue missions in Laos. A pilot could determine the magnetic direction and distance to or from this site. As we flew over the Skyline TACAN station, I looked out and down and saw a large lake on our lower right side.

Just a few months before, when I flew H-53 Jolly Greens from Udorn, I came in this direction when heading to Long Thien, Laos, which was Laotian Gen. Vang Pao's headquarters. He was a good guy. The big difference was, it was daytime then, and I could talk to people. Normally, this part of Laos was relatively safe. There were no MIG airfields or SAM sites to worry about--not yet, anyway. After an hour and a half of flying, it was time to begin our air-to-air refueling. The HC-130, Lime 1, piloted by Maj. Bill Kornitzer, was holding a steady platform. The refueling drogue hoses were extended on both sides of the HC-130. Each 75-foot hose had a white chute- type device on its end, and they were normally stable unless you were in turbulence. I completed our pre- refueling checklist items, which included extending our refueling probe just outside of our H-53 rotor plane. No external spotlight was used, as was the normal nighttime procedure. Apples 1 and 2 both took on their fuel. Then, we were next. Marty moved our H-53 toward the HC-130 drogue. He moved in slightly, and we connected with the drogue. I leaned forward to confirm fuel

116

transfer from the HC-130, and in a few minutes we filled our tanks. I told Marty, "Sir, we are full."

"Roger," he replied.

We backed off and resumed our formation position. We had enough fuel to get us to Son Tay POW camp and possibly all the way home. At least we could refuel in a safe area later if needed. If we did need more fuel before landing, it would be a cinch. On the way back, we could talk to the C-130 tanker and use external lights if needed. Apples 4 and 5, and Banana refueled on the left side.

We were rapidly approaching the border of North Vietnam and enemy radar coverage. It was time to change our C-130 lead. Lime 1 climbed ahead and then turned to the west where he would orbit in case he was needed to provide more fuel to the helicopters. Sliding over from our left was the MC-130, called "Blackbird", an aircraft with several nicknames. His call sign was Cherry 1. A sister ship, Cherry 2, was escorting the five A-1 "Peach" assault support aircraft.

They were somewhere nearby and would meet us at Son Tay so the A-1s could provide close air support near the POW camp. Once again, our big brothers would be there to protect us.

I had no idea what procedures the radar navigators on board the MC-130 used to get us around the enemy radar sites. That way, if I was captured, I couldn't be forced to answer a question I didn't know the answer to. We were less than an hour west of our objective. Our flight direction began to change--right, then left, dodging enemy radar detection patterns. Apple 3 was on the outside of the formation on the right side. We turned eastward and descended near a mountain range on our right. I looked at the trees, and our rotor blades were just clearing them.

"Marty," I said, "those trees are pretty darn close on the right side!"

"Roger that," he said. (I thought we were making toothpicks.)

The assault group--the MC-130s with the assault helicopters, and the other MC-130 with the A-1s, descended into the Da River valley (Black River) west of Hanoi. I saw bright lights from Hanoi like no one there was asleep. Our Navy had launched their planned diversion attack jets out in the Gulf of Tonkin, but I couldn't see any activity from our altitude. The MC-130 turned to place us near the initial point (IP), which was some 11 miles west of our target. All was still quite.

We descended toward our planned breakup point, some three and a half miles west of Son Tay. I looked outside the window but saw no houses or buildings, just trees, bushes, and rice paddies. I could barely see the Hong River (Red River). It flows through North Vietnam from the northwest to the southeast and goes through Hanoi and out to the Gulf of Tonkin. A small tributary comes off the main river and flows just west of the Son Tay POW camp. That small branch was what I was looking for, since it is just in front of the target. USAF and USN fighter pilots created a select group called the Red River Valley Fighter Pilots Organization. To belong, you had to fly a mission over the Red River. Hell, we were almost in the damn thing. I suspect the fighter jocks never planned to fly at 40 feet and 20 knots, and then land and wait in a hostile area for another twenty minutes or so.

The time for Apple 3 to assume lead position of the assault helicopter formation during the final tract to the target came up fast. Cherry 1, our lead MC-130, gave a heading of 072 degrees over the radio, the first time that radio silence was broken. They began a climb to 1500 feet and continued to the POW camp to drop their four flares over "Barbara". Marty looked at me and said he was going left another five degrees to 067. That should place us just to the left of the camp, as we had discussed, and place us in a better attack mode. Apples 4 and 5 climbed and followed the MC-130; they would act as alternates to drop flares if needed. We slowed down to between 75-80 knots so that Banana and Apples 1 and 2 could get into trail formation behind us and slightly to our right side. Without external lights, PJ Sgt. Angus Sowell, could not see the helicopters from our rear ramp platform. Cyclone Patsy's projected high winds would be coming from our left, or north, and would cause us to drift further southward.

I looked out my front and side windows to make sure there were no unknown obstacles such as big trees or power poles. We were still descending. Prior to attacking the camp gun towers, we were to level at 40 feet and fly at about 20-25 knots as we crossed the compound to take out the two gun towers. It was still dark and, even though the moon was higher, I couldn't see any significant features such as buildings or rivers. Then I heard on the radio, "Alpha, Alpha, Alpha," a transmission from Cherry 1. I looked at my watch, and it was 0217local. Suddenly, the sky lit up, and I could see. The flares from Cherry 1 provided excellent vision of the immediate area. Marty and I scanned out front for key reference points, like the river running in front of the camp. We both looked out front and saw a facility out there, but there was no river running from north to south just to the west of it.

"That is not it!" I yelled at Marty. "No river!"

I looked to our left and saw the target. "There it is," I said, pointing my left hand toward the left side or to the north.

Marty saw it, gave a big "Roger that," and began a steep turn to the left. I looked out my right window and saw what I believed to be the H-3, Banana. He appeared to be in a left turn as if he was following us. I told Marty what I saw and asked him if he wanted to break radio silence.

"No!" he said.

The extra drift correction we applied to our heading was still not enough to keep us from drifting to the right. Cyclone Patsy's winds were even stronger than the weather folks had projected for this area and altitude. The winds from our left were very strong. They pushed us a quarter mile right of course in three and a half miles of flying. If we had used the 072 heading that was given, we would be further to the south, somewhere below the secondary school. Marty's analysis was correct.

We were in a perfect position to continue our attack. Then, one of the worst things that could happen in a helicopter, happened. A yellow caution light illuminated just in front of me. It lit up the whole cockpit. Marty was still lining up for our mini-gun attack, and I leaned forward and saw that the light was the main gear transmission warning light. It illuminated if any metal pieces were floating around in our main transmission gearbox. They make contact and send a signal to our warning light in the cockpit; or, it could be just a circuit malfunction. I remembered something from my recent past. About six months ago, while flying at NKP on a training flight, we were on the ground, and I saw a similar light come on. We taxied in and parked the helicopter. The crew chief climbed up and found many metal pieces. He told us it was good we were here on the ground and had shut down the engines, because the transmission was about to explode.

If a transmission warning light comes on during flight, the H-53 flight manual instructs the pilot to pull out the circuit breaker, wait, and reset it. If the caution light goes out, then you can continue flight, but should monitor it. However, if the warning light stays on, then you need to land as soon as possible and have the transmission checked out by your crew chief. I reset the light, and the light stayed on.

Marty said, "Forget it. Leave the circuit breaker out."

We may be hitching a ride back ourselves, I thought to myself. I hoped one of the other H-53s had room for five more passengers. It was a long way back to friendly places, and I didn't want to become a new resident of North Vietnam. Marty continued to maneuver Apple 3, lining us up right on the centerline of the compound. So far, no one was shooting at us. We were not wearing our chest protectors, since they were protecting the Claymores. Our gunners, Hodges, Rogers, and Sowell, were on their guns. In just a few seconds, they would open fire at both gun towers. Adios, bad guys! The Yanks are here!

Our flight engineer, Paul Hodges, was on the mini-gun out the crew entry door on my side of the H-53. When our crew studied the camp mockup, Hodges told me that after he took out the enemy gun tower, he was going to take out the buildings just outside of the walls, since North Vietnamese soldiers were probably in there. As our H-53 crossed the western compound wall, all hell broke loose. Our mini-guns began to blaze away as advertised from the door and the window sides and, soon after, the rear ramp. Three mini-guns were firing up to 4,000 rounds per minute each. We were certainly leaving a lot of lead to clean up and a few fires were breaking out. Even though I was looking ahead for obstructions, I could see buildings blazing away out my right window.

We flew down the POW camp at 40 feet and 25 knots. Then, PJ Jim Rogers on the left window mini-gun position selected the intra-plane frequency so that Banana H-3 could hear and be alerted: "Man loose in compound." Jim said he saw a guy climbing down the tower ladder into the compound. He fired into the thatched roof of the tower to make sure the guy was out, and wouldn't be able to fire his machine gun from the tower. PJ Sowell did not have to fire his M-60, and he was back on his ramp mini-gun and opened fire.

Behind us was Banana with his 14-man Blueboy element that also opened fire on the guard in the compound before they landed. Apple 3 cleared the end of the camp, and I saw Hanoi out in front about 23 miles.

I went on the interphone and asked Marty, "Are we going to visit Hanoi?"

"Oh shit," he said and quickly reversed our course about 180 degrees.

We flew back on the north side of the camp and found a landing spot less than a mile from the camp. My heart was still pumping and the adrenaline machine was on maximum output, when I heard on our radio, "Plan Green". It was less than five minutes into the mission. What happened? "Plan Green" meant that Apple 2 had landed at the POW camp landing zone, and there was no sign of the

Greenleaf element from Apple 1. What happened to Apple 1? Where was he? I heard no distress call.

Marty and I looked out our windows, and we couldn't see any type of aircraft burning. There had been no emergency call made by Apple 1. Where were they?

After the Army Redwine element disembarked from Apple 2, Lt. Col. Allison's H-53 took off again and landed to the right of us in the rice paddy about 30 feet away. I could see them clearly.

Our two jet engines were set at flight idle to reduce our fuel consumption and lower our sound level. The wait began as Blueboy element began going cell to cell to free the prisoners, using their bolt cutters to open each cell. They would lead the ITEMS over to the south wall, which would be blown open soon. They were to wait there before being loaded onto Apple 4 and Apple 5 and, finally, on Apple 3. We were their ticket home, pre-paid and ready. The next call we heard should be for Apple 4 to come in and load ITEMS. When they departed, Apple 5 would come in, load, and depart. Then, we would go in and clear out whoever remained. We were ready.

Just then, PJ Jim Rogers came on our interphone. "Sir, with our night-vision starlight scope, I see a truck just to the north, parked along the road. I see a few guys walking around, and they seem to be looking our way."

Marty looked at me and said, "Tom, check it out."

I unstrapped quickly, stepped down, and went over to the window behind Marty's seat. I squatted down and peeked through the starlight scope. Damn, there **was** a truck parked there, and I saw two guys walking around. I couldn't tell if they had rifles. Could they see us? Did they hear our engines turning? They sure looked close. Then, the two guys climbed back into their truck and moved out. They were gone. Wow, that was close! The PJs continued to scan for other unwanted visitors--those with guns that might try to sneak up on us and start shooting.

Suddenly, all hell broke loose. Marty and I saw many SAMs launched from the north and east. It began to look like the Fourth of July. A lot of friendly MIGCAP fighters, F-4s, and F-105s, were flying high above us, so there were many targets for the SAMS. Even though many SAMs went up, no one had been hit so far. I had not heard any "Bandit" calls on our emergency frequency, which would announce any MIG launches.

To our left and on the deck was a fast moving jet with his afterburner lit. Who the hell is that? Was it a MIG? Was it one of our F-105s? Guess we will never know.

Less than ten minutes into the mission, I heard a radio transmission from the Blueboy element inside the POW camp: "Wildroot, this is Blueboy, Negative ITEMS." (Wildroot was Col. Simon's personal call sign)

I looked at Marty with a "what did he say" look on my face. Then, a call came from another Army element. "Blueboy, repeat your transmission, over." "Roger, this is BLUEBOY. I say again, Negative ITEMS!"

Marty and I looked at each other with our stomachs in our boots. "Did he say no one is there?" I asked.

Marty responded, "Sure sounds like it."

"Damn," I said. "We came all this way, and there is no one here? The plan worked, and we would have gotten them all out."

"I don't think the bad guys knew we were coming," Marty said, "they would have blown us all right out of the sky."

He was right. There were too many sitting ducks for the North Vietnamese soldiers to shoot out of the sky: six helicopters, five A-1s, and a couple of big C-130s, all at low level and flying very slowly. That would have given them a big news film, and perhaps even Hanoi Jane would show up.

In all of this commotion, I suddenly saw Apple 1 land next to Apple 2. "Col. Britton's back!" I told Marty on the interphone. Where had they been during the past ten minutes? They dropped off their Army Greenleaf element, but, since no POWs where at the camp, Apple 1 would get the call to load the 22-man Greenleaf element and part of the Blueboy/Banana crew.

About 0230 the Army unit called for Apple 1 to come into Barbara's landing zone and load up. In addition Col. Simon's Greenleaf element, there were now 14 more soldiers, the Blueboy element, plus the three Air Force crewmen who had flown into the POW camp on the H-3. All would be divided up for a ride home on Apple 1 or Apple 2. (Banana H-3 was to be blown up shortly after all friendly forces departed.) Shortly, Apple 1 was loaded, and they left the area heading west.

Then Firebird 3, an F-105, was hit by a SAM and made a Mayday call. No one bailed out. Our radios were getting busy. Apple 2 was called in to get the remainder of the raiders. Where the hell were our prisoners? We came all this way to take them home, and they had been moved? It was getting busy out there. We might have a Search and Rescue mission for the F-105 crew if they bailed out.

Apple 2 landed south of the camp, and the remaining raiders began to get on board. Soon, Apple 2 departed. Then Apple 1 and Apple 2 had to check how many souls were on board. If everyone was accounted for, we could depart. It was time to head west and haul our butts back to good guy land. On the FM frequency, I heard Apple 1 and Apple 2 talking about how many men were on their helicopters.

"Count is incorrect," was the response on the radio.

Marty called Apple 1. "Sir, Apple 3. Do youwant us to go in and pick up anyone who was left behind?"

"Standby, Apple 3," Lt. Col Britton replied. Confusion reigned. Did someone not count correctly--56 Army and 3 Air Force crewmen loaded on the two H-53 helicopters? Meanwhile, all of the other aircraft--Apples 1, 2, 4, and 5, our cover A-1s, and the two MC-130s--were leaving Dodge-all except us. We were still sitting there in the damn rice paddy with our engines set for takeoff power; however, we were still waiting to see if someone, indeed, was left behind at the POW camp. If we needed to go back in to rescue someone, I would call the A-1s to come back and give us air cover. Marty and I had decided we were not going to leave anyone behind to be killed or captured.

Just then another "Mayday, Mayday" came over the radio guard channel. "This is Firebird 5. We are hit and will continue westward." Great, now another F-105 was hit. Who would get them if they bailed out? Us, Apple 4 or Apple 5?

After three minutes elapsed (it seemed like an hour), another radio message came: "Apple 3, the count is correct. You are cleared to depart the area."

"Roger," Marty replied as he pulled the collective lever up, and we began to rise from the rice paddy. Bye-bye, North Vietnam. We are out of here.

We lifted off, turned 180 degrees, and headed west. We flew down the rice paddy and stayed low as we built our airspeed. We hit 150 Indicated Airspeed, and popped up to a higher altitude, 1500 feet or so. A few minutes went by, and I heard our PJ on the rear ramp, Sgt Sowell: "Sir, looks like Banana helicopter just exploded inside the compound!" Well, that went as planned.

I relieved Marty at the flight controls. Out our left side, I could see, down low and behind us, some type of aircraft getting rid of ammo--certainly shooting at something, but not us. With Firebird 5 being hit, one of the HC-130 aircraft, Lime 2, would be the rescue commander if Firebird 5's crew bailed out and a search and rescue effort was needed.

About thirty minutes later, I heard that Firebird 5's crew had, indeed, bailed out and were near the SKYLINE TACAN. Lime 2 changed his call sign to King 2. The A-1s would change their call signs to Sandy Lead and 2, 3, 4, and 5 if needed. The Firebird rescue area was in a much better location than somewhere in North Vietnam. Since Apple 4 and Apple 5 were close to the rescue location, they continued on to air refuel and take up positions to rescue the downed pilot and navigator. Meanwhile, more rescue Jolly Greens were launched from Udorn Air Base to serve as backups for the Firebird 5 mission.

We were cleared to return to Udorn. We were in a safer area of Laos, so we turned on all of our internal lights. The main-gear transmission warning light circuit breaker was still not engaged. Finally, I was able to talk to someone in the aircraft control business.

I pushed my UHF channel button. "Udorn Approach Control, this is Apple 3, 30 miles north of Udorn, requesting direct approach for landing, over."

"Apple 3, you are cleared present position, direct to Udorn. Call on final. Change to tower frequency, over," came a friendly voice.

"Roger," I replied. On final I gave the tower our final gear down and locked call. The sky to the east was getting lighter, just like the song, "by the dawn's early light." We certainly saw many rockets' red glare a bit earlier. Doesn't get any better, except we don't have our valuable cargo. I don't remember another time in my life when I was so totally disappointed. We did not bring back any of the American Prisoners of War.

I made the landing and taxied to our parking spot adjacent to Apple 1 and Apple 2. I parked the H-53 and shut down our engines. The mission was done.

I saw the various Army elements begin to load onto buses. Apple 1 and Apple 2 flight crews were sitting on the ramp in front of their helicopters. We gathered our gear and left our H-53. Our crew chief came over, and Marty told him about the main gear transmission light coming on. He climbed up to check it out.

"Looks OK to me," he said. We dodged a big one!

I saw a medic from an ambulance treating someone. It appeared to be the flight engineer from Banana, TSgt. Leroy Wright. His foot was wrapped. I did not see anyone among the Army elements or any other Air Force crewmen being treated by medics or being carried away. It looks like we entered the gates of Hell, and came back all in one piece. We were just missing our precious cargo, very special brothers-in- arms. Maybe next time, guys.

As I had taxied to our parking spot, I had seen a T-39, a small jet transport, parked nearby. I saw someone talking to Apple 1's crew, and everyone was standing. Then he walked over to Apple 2, and they, too, stood up and saluted. Then, in the dawn's early light, I could make out the figure. It was Gen. Leroy Manor, our overall mission commander. We stood when he approached and gave him a salute. He returned the salutes and told us to relax. He shook each hand and told us how much he appreciated our heroic efforts. He shared our disappointment in not bringing home our POWs. He was a busy man, and in a short time, he would head back to Washington to brief the Secretary of Defense and President Nixon. Yet, he took the time to greet each raider, one by one. He was a true leader. What could I learn from a leader like Gen. Manor? That everyone on a mission is important and should be recognized. Without dedicated professionals, the best equipment in the world won't do a thing. Thank you, General Manor, for being a true leader.

To complete the mission, word came down that both of the downed crewmen from Firebird 5 were rescued by Apple 4 and Apple 5. No one was injured.

As I walked over to operations to turn in my weapons and other gear, I noticed two C-141 Medical Transport aircraft parked near us. They were to take our POWs back home, but not today. We were reminded by the general's staff that the details of our mission were still classified, and not to talk to our comrades about any mission details. We debriefed, and went back to Tahkli Air Base on board the C-141s originally planned to transport the POWs.

On the ride back to Eglin AFB, Florida, I was sitting next to TSgt. Leroy Wright. He reached inside his flight suit and pulled out a small, black, rectangular piece of plastic. He turned it over, and I could see a serial number written on it.

"I just couldn't leave this behind on the H-3 that was blown up," he said.

Of course, there was always a chance that, in the future, someone could go back into North Vietnam and try once again to bring back our POWs. So, we needed to keep the mission details secret. As we continued our flight home, I thought about a couple of questions that people might ask about our mission. One: why did you guys not go to another camp? Answer: I guess the planners assumed that once the element of surprise was over, you don't get another chance. By then, all the bad guys in North Vietnam would know you were in their hen house. Two: Was there a security leak?

Answer: I don't think I would still be around to write anything; there were too many sitting ducks for the bad guys not to fire upon. But, our USA Special Forces flat owned a few square miles of North Vietnam for about 20 minutes! God bless the Green Berets-glad they are on our side. It was great surrounded by all of those heroes.

CHAPTER XVII

FREE AT LAST

After the Thanksgiving holiday, my phone kept ringing. There were dozens of phone calls from friends and relatives. "Gee, you know, I can't really talk about it," was my standard reply. I think my H-53 students and old Jolly Green crewmembers were the worst. What happened? Were you shot at by SAMs? Where were the prisoners? Many questions, but no answers.

In December, the H-3 and H-53 Son Tay Raid helicopter crews stationed at Eglin were told we were to go to Fort Bragg, North Carolina, for an Awards and Decorations ceremony--Class A uniform, and families were invited. (Fort Bragg is the location of the Army Special Forces.) Since there were twenty of us plus wives and a few older kids, the USAF sent a C-130 to fly us from Eglin to Fort Bragg. Son David, now eight, even got to go into the cockpit and fly the airplane.

We formed up on a giant parade field, with the Army and Air Force recipients in two sections. Our families were seated in reviewing stands to the west of the field. The VIPs arrived in a military van. Several high-ranking Army and Air Force officers and a gentleman in a dark blue suit got out of the van and walked toward the recipients. To my left, someone said, "Wow, that's Secretary of Defense Melvin Laird!"

The awards team consisted of Secretary Laird, Gen. Manor, and several colonels. Another officer was at the mike and read the citation prior to the award. A few able men were carrying trays of medals. The awards team came down the ranks and awarded each member, the higher awards first.

Six Army members received the Distinguished Service Cross (only the Medal of Honor is higher), and the other 50 Army officers and NCOs received Silver Stars (two notches below the Medal of Honor).

Next, the team came to the USAF Son Tay assault crewmembers, which included the H-3, H-53, HC-130, A-1 pilots, and the MC-130 crews. Lt. Cols. Britton and Allison, Maj. Marty Donohue, Maj. Herb Kalen, and TSgt. Leroy Wright (all assault helicopter crew members) received the Air Force Cross, one notch below the Medal of Honor. Receiving Silver Stars were the A-1, Peach pilots, the remaining Banana pilot, the remaining Apple crews, and several of the Cherry crewmembers. That day, I was surrounded by heroes, all in one place. It was rare to stand among over 90 other men holding the Silver Star and another 11 holding an award just below the Medal of Honor. I do not remember ever feeling as humbled as I did that day. Who were they? Why did they risk their lives for someone they did not know? Often in life, there are no easy answers to tough questions. We tried, but still missing were our POWs. Would we go back to another camp? We were ready. Would we see these Army Special Forces soldiers from Fort Bragg again? Following lunch we gathered all of the Eglin folks and headed back to Florida. It had been quite a day.

After returning to Eglin, things got back to normal. The ARRTC unit was to move from Florida to Utah. Another new instructor joined the Eglin group, my old friend Capt. Wade Weeks from Udorn. Then, just before moving to Utah, I got a phone call from Wright-Patterson AFB.

The major on the other end of the phone asked, "Capt. Waldron, where do you want to attend graduate school?"(No one in personnel had informed me that I was an alternate to go to graduate school via the Air Force group at Wright-Patterson AFB, Ohio.) My name came up, hence the phone call. A few hours later, I found myself and family changing our plans and heading to Columbia, Missouri, to attend civil engineering graduate school at the University of Missouri.

I was a tiger again! All of the younger students made fun of my slide rule. Computers? What are they, the old dinosaur (me) asked? While in school, I was presented a Congressional Award given to the Son Tay Raiders by the United States Congress. After 18 months (two football seasons), I completed my master's degree, and went to Mac Dill AFB in Florida to be a civil engineer and fly part time in the old T- bird (T-33, Lockheed's Shooting Star). We settled in, living on base at Mac Dill, home to many F-4 fighters. I was now Maj. Waldron, thanks to being promoted prior to checking into my new base.

The peace talks in France started to produce results. Beginning in February 1973, some of our prisoners of war in North Vietnam were being sent home. Before long, all of them came home. On April 4, 1973, the last C-141 lifted off from Hanoi and flew to Hickam AFB in Hawaii. Over 500 POWs were going to be reunited with their families, some after seven years or more in captivity. Thank God, they were free. It will take them a while to adjust to showers, real food, kids, and, yes, a wife. All those daily things we take for granted had been non-existent in their lives during the past few years, not to mention poor, if any, medical care.

Not long after, someone knocked on my small office door in the Civil Engineering Squadron. It was Mrs. Johnson, my new boss's (Col. Felix Fowler, an old F-86 pilot) secretary.

"Maj. Waldron (I was still not used to responding to that name), do you know a Mr. Ross Perot?" she asked.

"No, ma'am, not personally," I replied. "Why?" "Well, his secretary is on Col. Fowler's phone, and she wishes to speak with you."

Ross Perot? I had heard several stories of how he had helped the families of those men listed as Missing-in-Action and those held as POWs. He was a real patriot. And he had a few bucks lying around.

"Maj. Tom Waldron, ma'am," I said into the phone.

"Major, Mr. Perot is inviting you and your wife to San Francisco on April 26 and 27 for a welcome home parade for our returning American Prisoners of War, and he would like for the Son Tay Raiders to attend and also be in the parade. Hotel reservations have been made at the Fairmont Hotel in the Knob Hill section of San Francisco. I am sending you a package that has all necessary information. Are there any questions?"

"No ma'am. Thank you very much," was my shocked reply.

That evening as I went through the mail, I saw a personal letter from Mr. Perot inviting us to San Francisco for the parade. Of all places--home of the hippies and Vietnam War protestors. I guess those who planned this figured none of that crowd would dare mess with Special Forces soldiers. I sure as hell would not. It was a long flight on a TWA Boeing 707 (heck, I could fly a 707). We flew from Tampa to St. Louis, changed planes, and then continued to San Francisco.

Finally, I met some of the POWs. In the elevator a couple of the guys started talking about how they kept their minds going while being held captive. One said he built a

134

house, including drawing plans, all in his mind. Another said he memorized restaurants from the various towns the other POWs were from. Give him a category and city and he could tell you the location and type of food--Italian, Mexican, or whatever.

At times it was emotional. POWs would come up and give me a big hug and thank me for trying. I think that make everything OK. Many of the guys said that, after our raid, they were moved into Hanoi and allowed to have roommates, which helped them keep going. It had helped their morale knowing that their country still cared about them and tried to get them home.

Mr. Perot certainly did a lot for the families during this time. All of what went on was good, private, and not to be published. Our country is indeed fortunate to have a patriot like him.

I met a few of the Son Tay prisoners. One was Air Force Capt. Dave Ford (shot down in 1967); another was Lt. Col. Wes Schierman (shot down in 1965). They both had suffered many physical problems, and there were no doctors or clinics to help them heal injuries.

I asked Capt. Ford, "Where in the hell were you guys that early morning on November 21, 1970?"

He said, "A few months prior to the attack, the North Vietnamese guards told us that our well water supply was dry, and they moved us to another camp at night. Not sure how far away the new camp was from Son Tay, but the night of the raid, we heard the attack that early morning. We knew something big was going on. I think the prison guards were a bit rattled after that attack. Heck, you guys might come back!"

After a large parade winding through San Francisco, the POWs their families, and the Raiders came back to the hotel. That night we had a unique dinner and entertainment program. While I was standing there talking with some of the POWS (me in my cheap Sears suit), nursing a gin and tonic, in walked one of the invited guests--none other than John Wayne, the Duke.

I remember looking up and then shaking his hand. He said he was proud of all of the Raiders and POWs. John Wayne had always been Mr. Patriot in my world. Wow! Then, Mr. San Francisco himself, Clint Eastwood, along with his bride, came in. Our wives were now paying attention to the doorway. Red Skelton and the Andrews Sisters closed out the guest stars. Mr. Perot obviously knows the right people.

That was the first time both groups to gathered as one. Now, there have been several joint reunions held by the NAMPOWs (the Vietnam Prisoners of War Association) and, the Son Tay Raiders Association (STRA). The last joint reunion was in 2008, when Senator John McCain, a NAMPOW himself, was very busy running for President and could not make the Dallas reunion. Mr. and Mrs. Ross Perot hosted a great BBQ dinner outside on their ranch just west of Dallas. At that reunion, I noticed that even more of the POWs and Raiders were no longer with us. Twelve of our 28 helicopter crewmen had passed on by the fall of 2008. Several more were ill and could not travel.

When the war in Vietnam was over, many combat missions became declassified, including the Raid on Son Tay. In 1976, Benjamin F. Schemmer released a book called *The Raid*. He had access to many files, and suddenly the world knew what had happened to Apple 1 that early morning during the ten minutes that I had lost sight of them. They had landed at the "secondary school" with the Greenleaf group. A small war erupted and many enemy soldiers were killed. I was amazed that, for years, I did not know what had happened, and I worked next to some of these crewmen. They did their job in not talking.

A few conjectures came forward. One was that the strong winds blew Apple 1 further south off course, and they did not recognize they were at the wrong place until after they were there. With the battle going on, they had to finish the job there and then get back to the Son Tay POW camp. I still scratch my head about that. Apple 3, our helicopter, had dropped down and moved forward so that the H-3, Banana, and the other H-53s, Apple 1 and Apple 2, could follow us in trail formation. There were still no external lights turned on, and radio silence was still in effect.

I don't know how Banana and Apple 2 found the POW camp flying behind us, and Apple 1 did not. He should have been in front of Apple 2. Both pilots from Apple 1 are now deceased and so is most of their crew. The Army commander on board, Col. Simon, has also passed.

Our Son Tay group's 40th reunion of the raid was held in the Eglin AFB area in November 2010. On the agenda included a special memorial service led by Chaplain Gardner at a memorial park on Hurlburt Field, west of the Eglin AFB area. Hurlburt Field is still home to USAF Special Operations. The Son Tay Association President, Dan Turner, Redwine element, and several of the other Raiders, read the names of each of our fallen warriors, all 66 of them. This 40th reunion was special, since it was held at Eglin AFB, where much of our training before the raid had occurred. It is also the place where Col. Jimmy Doolittle trained his bomber crews before they bombed Japan in World War II.

In this book, I use the terms "guys" and "men" a lot. In 1969 and 1970, there were no women pilots, flight engineers, or PJs stationed in our rescue squadrons. I am sure if there had been, they would have served just as honorably. So, in the future, if you see a woman in a flight suit with a rescue patch, make sure you thank her for her service. Respect goes with the job and not the gender.

As I close this writing, I am often at odds on how to define a hero. Just who is a hero? I know there have been many books written about them-Audie Murphy and Jimmy Doolittle, for example. The heroes I was honored to fly with were everyday people, from small towns, farms, or even big cities. The common thread I saw was that when the situation demanded, one would rise above what might be considered by an outsider to be dangerous, yet, that person arose to do the job. In these cases, that usually involved saving another person's life-most often someone they did not know.

I would hope that, if relatives of some of these men who are now gone do research on their grandfather, uncle, or whomever, they see the type of person they are related to: a true hero.

Most of what I have written came from my personal notes and memory. I was indeed honored to have known each one I wrote about in the book.

EPILOGUE

There is a web site, **www.virtualwall.org** that names all aviators who are listed as Missing in Action or Killed in Action during the Vietnam War. There are continual updates based upon the recovery of human remains from data provided by field teams still searching known crash sites. The chapter updates below came from information on that web site.

BOXER 22-DECEMBER 1969

Earlier in the book, I talk about a three-day rescue mission that saved the life of an F-4 weapons officer, Lt. Woody Bergeron. On the second day of the mission, an Air Force Jolly Green PJ, Airman David Davison, was killed. He was awarded the Silver Star and Purple Heart.

The F-4 weapons operator, Lt. Bergeron, had heard gunshots during the first night, but that alone was not enough evidence to classify Boxer 22 A, who was Air Force Capt. Benjamin F. Danielson, as killed in action. It was not until 1976 that Capt. Danielson was classified as killed in action. In 2003, bone fragments matched DNA found at the crash site, according to information on the Vietnam Wall website.

PJ Doug Horka informed me that he escorted Airman Davison's sister and her husband to Kenyon, MN, to attend a memorial service for Capt. Danielson. Woody Bergeron was also in attendance. Finally, after many years, the family of Capt. Ben Danielson (Boxer 22 A), were able to bury his remains back home. Thanks, Doug-you always do the right thing.

BEEPER, BEEPER, COME UP VOICE

During the mission we flew on January 2, 1970, our crew had to leave the downed A-6 pilot's location after several 37mm anti-aircraft guns opened fire on us while we were in a hover. One of our PJs, Sgt. Rick Beasley, was on the ground attending a crewman in his parachute. We were forced to abandon our recovery. On a website www.angelfire.com, I found the names of the two downed USN A-6 crewmen: Lt. Bruce C. Fryar and Lt. Cmdr. Nicholas Brooks. We were unable to retrieve either of the two men during our aborted mission. Years later, Laotian freedom fighters found some remains that were identified as those of Lt. Cmdr. Brooks in 1982, and his remains were buried at sea. As of this writing, Lt. Fryar's remains have not been recovered.

BANDITS, BANDITS

The crew of Jolly Green 71, commanded by USAF Capt. Holly Bell, was shot down by a MIG 21 near the border of Laos and North Vietnam. According to the www.virtualwall.org web site, remains from Maj. Holly Bell were recovered in late 1988 and identified in June 1989. William Sutton's Military ID card and Geneva Convention card were also recovered.

The sixth man on the crew, Sgt. Gregory Anderson, belonged to the 600th Photo Squadron. A combat photographer, he also went down with the Jolly crew. The two F-105 crewmembers on Seabird02, had their partial remains returned in 1988.

LEROYS GONE

My friend, Capt. Leroy Schaneberg, and his crew's remains were identified, and returned in flag-draped coffins in 1995. They are buried in Arlington Cemetery in Washington, D. C.

WOMEN AND CHILDREN ONLY

I have never heard from anyone in Laos who was rescued that day from the hostile North Vietnamese Army fighting inside Laos. Some 40 years later, many of the adult ladies, then in their 30s or 40s, would be in their 70s or 80s. Little ones would not remember that day. Perhaps I'll never know how they fared.

SON TAY RAIDERS

We still gather every other year. At each reunion, we continue to have members leave this earth. Several detailed books have been written about the Son Tay Raid, including (in order of release):

The Raid by Benjamin F. Schemmer published in 1976.

The Son Tay Raid by John Gargus published in 2007. (John was on Cherry 1.)

Secret and Dangerous by William A. Guenon, Jr., published in 2002 and reprinted in 2005 and 2007. (William was the pilot on Cherry 1.)

GLOSSARY

A

AAA- Anti-aircraft artillery. Usually designated by shell diameter: 23mm, 37mm, etc.

AAM- Air-to-Air missile

AB- Air Base. Designation used in bases outside of the United States (e.g., Udorn Air Base)

AFB - Air Force Base. Designation used for air bases in the United States (e.g., Eglin AFB, FL)

AIRCRAFT- used in this book (order mentioned):

T-37/T-33: Cessna T-37 used in USAF Undergraduate Pilot Training (first six months).

Lockheed T-33 used in latter six months training.

KC-135-Boeing, four engine jet tanker flown by Strategic Air Command crews. Used for air-to-air refueling of the B-52, B-58 and B-47 bombers. Also used to air refuel Air Force fighter aircraft.

F-4-called the Phantom; manufactured by McDononnell Douglas. Used in Vietnam War as a strike aircraft, in MIGCAP protection, or as a forward air controller (call sign "Wolf").

F-100- Used in close air support of US Army troops. Also used as Forward Air Controller (FAC) (call sign "Misty").

F-105 - Called the Thud or Thunder Chief. Manufactured by Republic. Used to attack Surface-to- Air missile sites in North Vietnam. Also used in MIGCAP protection role and to bomb supply routes.

B-52- Boeing manufactured bomber flown by Strategic Air Command aircrews. Used to carpet- bomb by using several three-ship formations, dropping several hundred 500-pound bombs on each mission. Code name for missions: Arc Light. The bombers came, bombed, and left the area without talking to any aircraft controllers. Other aircrews had to know the Arc Light schedule and place of attack.

C-130- Manufactured by Lockheed and used in several missions: cargo, gunship, airborne command and control for search and rescue missions; provided air to air refueling for HH-3 and HH-53 USAF combat rescue helicopters. MC-130, called the "Blackbird," used in the Son Tay Raid   as escorts for assault helicopters and A-1 attack fighters.

UH-1- made by Bell; used in initial helicopter training.

HH-3 E- Sikorsky helicopter used in early combat rescue operations in Vietnam area. Gross weight of 20,000 pounds, 62-foot diameter main rotor, and two M-60 machine guns for aircrew defense. Air refueling capable with HC-130 (call sign: "Jolly xx").

HH-53- Sikorsky helicopter used in later combat rescue operations in Vietnam and Laos. Max weight of 40,000 pounds, 72-foot diameter main rotor, three six-barrel, 7.62mm mini-guns for aircrew defense. Air refueling capable with the HC-130 (call sign: "Jolly xx").

A-1- a propeller driven, single engine aircraft used by the USAF and USN during Vietnam/ Laos close support missions for troops on the ground and to protect survivors and helicopter crews during rescue operations (call sign for rescue missions: "Sandy x").

A-4-Douglas jet used by USN, along with the Grumman A-6, and LTV A-7. Note: Senator John McCain was shot down flying the A-4 over Hanoi.

ARRS-Aerospace Rescue and Recovery Service- Headquarters at Scott AFB, IL

ARRSq- Aerospace Rescue and Recovery Squadron (e.g., 40th ARRSq based in Udorn Air Base, Thailand

ARRTC- Aerospace Rescue and Recovery Training Center. In the late '60s and early '70s located at Eglin AFB, Fl. Aircrew/ground crew training in the H-43; H-3; H-53, and the C-130.

B

Bandits- Code word used to identify enemy MIG aircraft being launched in North Vietnam. Message given over two emergency radio channels: VHF (121.50) and UHF (243.0). Launch base and direction of the enemy flight path was given.

Barbara- Code name for the Son Tay POW compound mockup first seen by attack helicopter and A-1 aircrews at Hurlburt Field, Fl in late 1970.

Blood Chit- Laminated, plastic-coated document carried by aircrews on each combat flight. The document said "take this person to nearest US Embassy and get $100 in gold" in many Asian dialects. Each document had to be signed for and returned after each flight.

C

CIA- Central Intelligence Agency.

D

DMZ- Demilitarized Zone. Area between North and South Vietnam that runs along the Ben Hai River and was a few kilometers wide on each side.

F

FAC- Forward Air Controller. The aircrews usually flew O-1s/O-2s and OV-10s. Call signs were "Nail"/ "Raven". Each FAC pilot was assigned his personal flight call sign--e.g., Nail 34 was always Lt. Smith. At times the F-100 ("Misty" call sign) and F-4 ("Wolf" call sign) were used to direct airstrikes toward hostile ground forces.

FE-Flight Engineer. Each HH-3/53 Jolly Green helicopter had an FE crew position. During flight, the FE sat between the two pilots. During rescue operations, they operated the recovery hoist/jungle penetrator, which could reach a downed airman as much as 240 feet below the helicopter. FEs also could operate the H-3's M-60 aircrew weapon or the H-53's six-barrel 7.62mm mini-gun.

FM -Frequency Modulation. Radio frequency used by rescue helicopters and A-1 aircraft to coordinate future flight maneuvers involving exact rescue data, when to air refuel, etc.

H

Hotel- Code name for Hanoi, North Vietnam. MIGs were launched from airfields around Hanoi.

I

Ivory Coast- Code name for the Son Tay POW Raid (used during the planning/training phase).

IFF-Identification friend or foe-Black box in the plane that transmits pre-assigned codes to ground radar sites.

IFR- Instrument Flight Rules. Assigned route , departure, and approach/landing by a governing control-in USA it is Federal Aviation Agency.

J-Jolly Green- Call sign used by H-3 and H-53 rescue helicopters. Each assigned call sign to be used each flight by helicopter tail number: i.e., 68-8286 is "Jolly 65"). For the Son Tay Raid, each of the five H-53s used the mission-assigned call sign of "Apple" 1 through 5; the H-3 was "Banana".

Jungle penetrator- An electrical motor-operated hoist cable (240 feet) attached to the helicopter. The penetrator could bring up three crewmen on a given operation.

K

KIA- Killed in action.

King- Call sign used by the command and control HC-130 aircraft during rescue operations.

L

Lima Site- Small landing strips located throughout Laos. One used by the 40th ARRS was Lima Site 98, often called LS-20A. This was at Long Tieng in mid- Laos and often was not under friendly control. There, Jolly rescue crews were positioned an hour and a half closer to potential rescue missions in North Vietnam or central Laos.

M

MIA- Missing- in- action. Status of an individual used when it could not be determined if the individual was captured or killed.

MIG- Russian/Chinese fighters used by the North Vietnam aircrews. MIG 17, 19, and 21 models were used in the Vietnam War.

MIGCAP- Anti-MIG, combat air patrol. Designated aircrews (USAF/USN) trained and armed to provide protection for other friendly aircraft in the area.

N

NCO- Non Commissioned Officer, E-5 through E-9.

NIT-NOY - Means small in Thai language

NKP- Nakon Phanom Air Base, Thailand. Home air base of OV-1/2 and 10 FACs and A-1 aircraft, and some rescue helicopters. Often H-53s would spend the day and return to Udorn at night. Base is on the eastern border with Laos, and 90 miles from the North Vietnamese border.

NVA- North Vietnamese Army.

O

Ordinance- Aircraft armament such as guns, bombs, missiles, carried internally or externally under the wings.

P

Pathet Loa - Laotian enemy army forces that fought with the North Vietnamese forces.

PJ- A term used for the USAF pararescuemen. Select group of USAF airmen and NCOs who are qualified in life-saving water rescue, jump qualified, and medically trained in life saving procedures. Two PJs on each crew would operate the H-3/H-53 machine guns. Often they would go on the jungle penetrator to assist a downed, wounded airman.

POW or PW- Prisoner of War.

R

Ranks

US Air Force Enlisted		US Army Enlisted	
Chief Master Sergeant	CMsgt	Command Sergeant Major	CSM
Senior Master Sergeant	SMsgt	Sergeant Major	SGM
Master Sergeant	Msgt	First Sergeant	1SG
Technical Sergeant	Tsgt	Master Sergeant	MSG
Staff Sergeant	Ssgt	Sergeant First Class	SFC
Senior Airman	SrA	Staff Sergeant	SSG
Airman First Class	A1c	Sergeant	SGT
Airman	Amn	Corporal	CPL
Airman Basic	AB	Specialist	SPC

Ranks: Officer Flying types – Pilots/Navigators

Air Force Officers		Navy Flight Officers	
Colonel	COL	Captain	CAPT
Lieutenant Colonel	LT COL	Commander	CDR
Major	MAJ	Lieutenant Commander	LCDR
Captain	CAPT	Lieutenant	LT
First Lieutenant	1LT	Lieutenant Junior Grade	LTJG
Second Lieutenant	2LT	Ensign	ENS

S

SAC- Strategic Air Command. SAM- Surface-to-Air Missile.

Sandy- Call sign used by A-1 fighters during search and rescue missions. Each Jolly Green had two Sandys assigned for their protection.

SAR- Search and Rescue. SEA- Southeast Asia.

SFG- Special Forces Group.

SIF- Selective Identification Feature(used in conjunction with the IFF feature.

Son Tay- Remote city some 23 nautical miles northwest of Hanoi, North Vietnam, that had a POW compound just south and west of the city, near the river.

Son Tay Raid call signs :

> Air Force Assault group one: MC-130=Cherry1, HH-3 Helicopter=Banana; HH-53= Apples 1 through 5.

> Group Two: MC-130=Cherry 2; A-1s=Peach 1 through 5.

> Special Forces: 14 men in Banana (Blueboy); Apple 1, 22 men (Greenleaf); Apple 2, 20 men

> (Redwine). Col Simon= Wildroot.

SOS- Special Operations Squadron.

T

TAC- Tactical Air Command.

Tahkli Air Base- One of seven USAF bases in Thailand. Son Tay Raiding Force was there two days before launching to Udorn Air Base.

TACAN- Tactical Air Navigation system, which provides direction and distance in nautical miles to or from the selected station. Often the position of a downed airman was given using TACAN location (e.g., "Seabird 02 down, location is 090 [degrees] at 92 nautical miles from Channel 95").

TDY- Temporary Duty. Official orders designate the location and time of remote duty from home base.

TFW- Tactical Fighter Wing. TFS- Tactical Fighter Squadron. Thud- Nickname for the F-105.

U

Udorn Air Base- Air Force Base in Northern Thailand about thirty miles south of Laotian border. Home of the 40th ARRSq (HH-53s), the 481st TFW (F-105s), and Air America aircraft (CIA).

USAF- United States Air Force. USN- United States Navy.

V

VHF- Very High Frequency (30 to 150 MHz).

ILLUSTRATIONS

F105s in formation

KC-135 refuelingF105

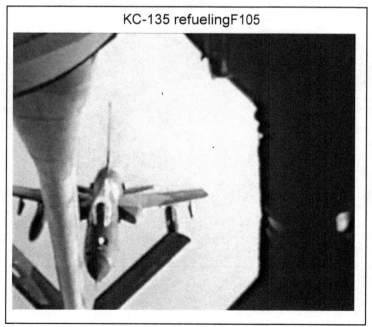

New Jolly Greens: H53, August 1969.
Back row: Waldron, Eastman, King, Nelson, Glass,
Turbyfield, Schaneberg, Gill . Front row: Martin,
Olsen, Van Brunt, Hutsch, (?,) Thurman, Colburn

H-53 tail gun- Sgt. Wayne Fisk (
courtesy of Jim Rogers)

(picture above courtesy of Doug Horka
photo after Boxer 22 attempt)
Another view of Jolly Green 79's battle damage,
as seen from outside and below while
parked on the ramp at NKP

Photos from Boxer 22 Bravo
From the personal achieves of Douglas L Horka
Survivor Boxer 22 Bravo
1st Lt. Woodrow Bergeron Jr
(Center frame beneath the hoist.)

Lt. Col. Lyle's Last Flight at NKP
(author Tom Waldron in door area)

(Left, front to rear: Heeter, Brown, Thompson,
Livengood, Kinsinger, unknown Right, front to rear:
Waldron, Brown, ?, Barber, Martin, Scoggins)

photo courtesy of Jim Rogers –
C130 air refueling H-53 en route to Lima Site

photo- courtesy of Jim Rogers
H-53 pilots Lt .Col York and Maj. Marty Donohue
Lima Site, Central Laos

(photo courtesy of Jim Rogers)
Air America Pilatus Porter Turbo
Prop taking off from Lima Site

(photo courtesy of Jim Rogers)
Air America H34 departing Lima Site

Son Tay, Apple 3, Gunship crew, November 1970:
left to right: Hodges, Donohue, Waldron, Sowell, Rogers
Donohue awarded the Air Force Cross,
the other four received Silver Stars.

Son Tay Raiders from ARRTC, Eglin AFB standing
in front of H53 – note the H-3 in background.
Back row: Tasker, Wright, Montgomery, McLoud,
Wellinton, Waldron, Allison, Britton
Front row: Galde, Rogers, Leeser, Hodges, Donohue

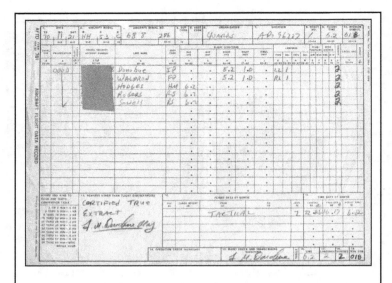

Flight record form 781 from Apple 3

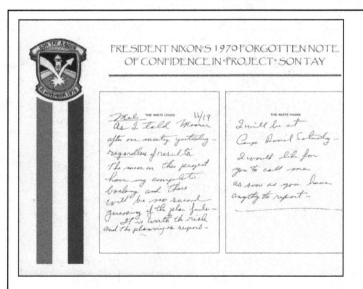

Note from President Nixon to Secretary to Defense
Melvin Laird, November 19, 1970.

MAPS

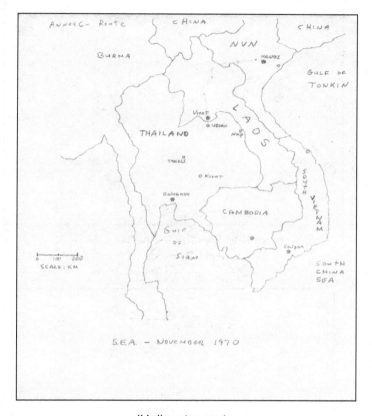

'Helicopter route-
Udorn AB to Son Tay POW camp.

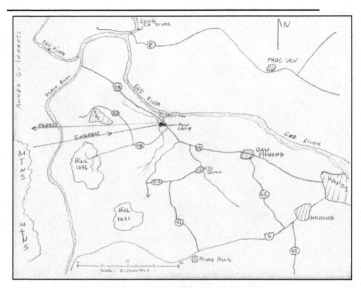

**Final Approach to Son Tay POW Camp-MC-130
with H-3/H-53s**

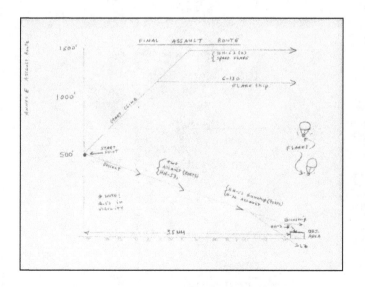

Last 3.5 Miles , 500 feet to 50 feet-Gunship H-53

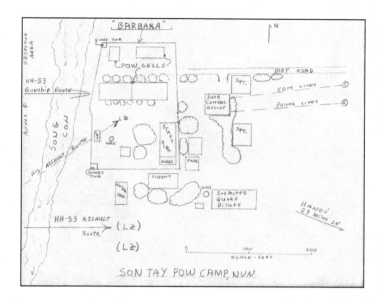

Display Of Helos at Son Tay POW Camp Area
Apple 3-Gunship; Apples 1 and 2 with USA Special Forces
Assault troops . H-3 Banana landing inside camp.

CPSIA information can be obtained
at www.ICGtesting.com
Printed in the USA
LVHW022132170321
681813LV00036B/1061